GO BEYOND BOUNDS

BEING A GLOBAL ENTREPRENEUR

SHASHIDHAR JAKKALI

STARDOM BOOKS

WORLDWIDE

www.StardomBooks.com

STARDOM BOOKS

A Division of Stardom Publishing

and infoYOGIS Technologies.

105-501 Silverside Road

Wilmington, DE 19809

Copyright © 2017 by Stardom Publishing.

All rights reserved, including right to reproduce this book or portions thereof in any form whatsoever.

FIRST EDITION MAY 2017

Stardom Books

Go Beyond Bounds: Being a Global Entrepreneur/ Shashidhar Jakkali.

p. cm.

1. Business / Self-help / Motivation I. Title

ISBN-13: 978-1548110192

ISBN-10: 1548110191

DEDICATION

To my caring wife Rekha and loving daughters Nidhi & Sharadhi who have been strongest supporters in my entrepreneurial journey!

DISCLAIMER

The views, opinions and information presented in this book are from the co-authors of the publication. The publisher does not endorse or subscribe to the information; reader discretion is solicited.

This book is designed to provide information on how each one of the co-authors did what they did, as their own personal narrative. It is sold with the understanding that neither the co-authors nor the publisher is engaged in rendering legal, accounting or other professional services. If legal or other professional advice is warranted, the services of an appropriate professional should be sought. Also, this book cannot be an exhaustive and complete presentation on the topics within the book. While every effort has been made to make the information presented here as complete and accurate as possible, it may contain errors, omissions or information that was accurate as of its publication but subsequently has become outdated by marketplace or industry changes or conditions, new laws or regulations, or other circumstances.

Neither the co-authors nor the publisher accepts any liability or responsibility to any person or entity with respect to any loss or damage alleged to have been caused, directly or indirectly, by the information, ideas, opinions or other content in this book. If you do not agree to these terms, you should immediately return this book for full refund.

Foreword

I was pleasantly surprised when Shashidhar told me that he is recording his views on his journey as a global entrepreneur and publishing this as a book. He is very shy person and does not like to speak of himself. Therefore, it must have been a very deep desire to describe his journey as an entrepreneur so that it would help others make sense of his journey and capitalize on his experiences. Everybody's life- even the dullest one- holds some interesting aspect for others. A global entrepreneur who builds up his life and career from grounds-up will therefore be a great journey to follow. Shashidhar is just that sort of entrepreneur: An entrepreneur who was born and brought-up in the bowls of the security and semi-poverty of the Indian middleclass, but transcended both to start his journey as a global entrepreneur. His childhood makes for very interesting reading and shows glimpses of what follows. His uncertain and migrant early teens have prepared him to be proactive, rather than reactive in his transactions. Yet, this journey is far from over and he is still at it. A future version of this book is likely to be even more interesting as the premise raised here will show its natural conclusion there.

One of Mahatma's favourite is a quote attributed to the Buddha: "Happiness is a journey and not a destination" which he rewrote as: "The journey is more important than the destination". Shashidhar's journey is more valuable than the successes he may have achieved or which may have eluded him. Another famous writer, Ralph Waldo Emerson, famously said: "What lies behind us and what lies before us are tiny matters compared to what lies within us". Shashidhar exemplifies a great practical example of a person who has manifested this. His background or the uncertain and fuzzy future has been transcended by him. His exemplary journey alone is of interest to him. The results are of course to be expected. But preoccupation with the result, and not concentrating on execution of a perfect journey, will destroy both the thrill of the journey as well as the efficacy of the result. This is Shashidhar's current philosophy, firmly rooted in the oriental philosophies he enjoys reading.

I wish Shashidhar a great success with this book as well as to readers who may find it useful in their contexts. I also wish that he comes out with more such books as he progresses on his journey towards being a successful global entrepreneur.

Kumar Munipalli
Bangalore, India
14th April, 2017

Note From The Author

A short note about 'Arctic Tern' bird featured on the front of the book and its relevance to the title of the book and my entrepreneurial journey.

Reference article:
https://www.allaboutbirds.org/guide/Arctic_Tern/lifehistory

> Arctic Tern: A small, slender white bird, the Arctic Tern is well known for its long yearly migration. Its travel from its Arctic breeding grounds to its wintering grounds off of Antarctica may cover perhaps 40,000 km (25,000 mi), and is the farthest yearly journey of any bird.

SHASHIDHAR JAKKALI, AUTHOR

CONTENTS

1	REALIZING A DREAM OF GLOBAL ENTREPRENEURSHIP	BY SHASHIDHAR JAKKALI	1
2	GROUND ZERO	BY PHIL BRITTEN	15
3	THE CONTRARIAN RULE – CONTRARIAN ALWAYS WIN!	BY C T PARUN	25
4	ARE THE MESSENGER WHO TRANSFORMS LIVES	BY DR. JOANNE MESSENGER	33
5	DETOX AND DE-STRESS THROUGH LAUGHTER - THE STORY OF HASOVAN	BY SAVITHA HOSMANE	45
6	ARCHITECTING HEALTHY FAMILIES	BY SUNITHA SRIKANTH	61
7	HOW I GOT MY SUPERPOWERS AND CREATED MY IDEAL LIFE	BY JOHANN NOGUEIRA	71
8	MY PATH TO FREEDOM AND PURPOSE	BY LISA SCOLNICK	87
9	WHY I FAILED 541 TIMES?	BY VISHWANATH KOKKONDA	99
10	THE WORLD IS AT YOUR FOOTSTEPS	BY AMIT PUNJABI	109
11	THE PATH TO STOCK MARKET SUCCESS	BY ADRIAN REID	119
12	A FASTER WAY TO CREATE THE RESULTS YOU WANT IN LIFE & BUSINESS…WITH THE FA²ST SYSTEM™	BY GLENN DIETZEL	135
13	HOW TO CREATE DEMAND FOR YOURSELF AS A HIGHLY PAID SPEAKER, PRESENTER OR CONSULTANT EVEN IF YOU DON'T THINK YOU'RE AN EXPERT!	BY CYDNEY O' SULLIVAN	153
14	ON PARENTING, EDUCATION, AND THE FUTURE	BY AMI DESAI	173
15	ARE YOU JUMPING OUT OF BED IN THE MORNING?	BY DIANA DENTINGER	187
16	IMBIBING QUALITY AS A WAY OF LIFE	BY VANISHREE P ACHARYA	195
17	HOW CONSULTATIVE FINESSE BEATS TYPICAL FIGHT VS. FLIGHT IN STRESSFUL WORK SITUATIONS	BY ROLF FOSTER-JORGENSEN	203

ACKNOWLEDGMENTS

I am grateful to all the teachers and gurus in my life who have come in many different forms and figures to make me learn the value of every small thing that has happened, happening and yet to happen. My current personality is the end result of all the experiences I have accumulated so far.

Every step of the way I have been hand-held and smoothly taken from one situation to the next by the almighty thereby leaving rich experiences for me to cherish. I am grateful to that force and the ultimate consciousness, responsible for everything that is manifested and un-manifested.

1

REALIZING A DREAM OF GLOBAL ENTREPRENEURSHIP

- BY SHASHIDHAR JAKKALI, FOUNDER & CEO, AXIOM HEALTH INTELLECT SYSTEMS INC., CO-FOUNDER, LET'S START INCUBATION CENTER & FOUNDER, BLOCKENABLE

Unless you are born into a family-owned business, the transition from being just an employee working for an organization to becoming an entrepreneur aiming to build a global business is an extremely challenging task. Then the entrepreneurial journey itself is a long-drawn-out battle with no guarantee of winning. A battle within oneself, and with others. You may have the capital, skill-sets, a great team, even a good product idea, but unless Providence decides to stand by you, you do not stand much of a chance. Tangible requirements and good fortune are the two pillars for entrepreneurial success. Therefore, if there is one quality that goes into making an entrepreneur, it is Perseverance. One has to patiently wait until things start working in your favor.

To launch myself as an entrepreneur was not an easy decision. And once I made the decision, it was a precipice fall of sorts from a very comfortable life in Dubai to an anxiety-ridden life in Bangalore. At that time, I was the regional head of Middle East region for a well-established healthcare IT Company within a High-Tech, free-zone called Dubai Internet City. My family and I had settled down very comfortably into a lifestyle that had a little disturbance. Although I always desired to be an entrepreneur, certain complacency had set in and I was reluctant to change my lifestyle. Then an incident occurred. Few years into the job, I had a major difference of opinion with the management, which acted as a trigger for me to take one of the most difficult career decisions. I put in my papers. The management panicked for I was their earliest and best-performing employee. They offered prestigious job profiles and locations that I could head. Well, my mind was clear about what I wanted to do. I moved on and landed in Bangalore on a warm April morning of 2008.

Entrepreneurial Journey - Phase 1

The coward dies a thousand times before his death;
But the valiant tastes death but once.
                         - William Shakespeare

Upon my return to Bangalore, I launched a healthcare software product company in the field of data analytics, a specialized domain which was emerging globally as the next big technology revolution and soon it was named, 'Big-Data'. I was highly ambitious and wanted to establish a globally respected innovative software product company and my vision document was a killer of a kind all the way from building a cross-continental, multi-culture team up to the ambitious NASDAQ listing. The initial phase was very difficult. I was steeped in financial problems and I went through the entire cycle of wondering if I had done the right thing, or whether the timing was right, of feeling guilty of putting my family through all sorts of stress and so on. However, there is never a right moment. I have read somewhere, 'Don't wait for the perfect moment. Take the moment and make it perfect.' An opportunity lost is more expensive when compared to a temporary phase of instability.

Guiding principle for an entrepreneur that I saw in a Washington DC subway station

I had developed an innovative data analytics product idea to address one of the teething problems in the global healthcare industry. In the healthcare industry, software applications from different vendors run independently and one has to struggle to integrate disparate healthcare data thus generated, to correlate and arrive at a logical solution. We developed a common data analytics product platform that could assimilate diverse nature of healthcare data to create a seamlessly integrated intelligent solution. For instance, chronic disease management such as Cancer Treatment involves multiple technologies from different vendors and there was no common healthcare IT platform to assemble the data from disparate sources. It was an onerous task to bring-inthe data from different data sources and yet the result was unsatisfactory and too much time-consuming. Our product platform integrated all the chronic disease management data to arrive at an integrated solution and also took much shorter time to provide the insights into patient's disease condition and treatment path. What we offered were boutique solutions for every problem but on a common data analytics product platform.

However, soon after launching my company in June 2008, Global Financial industry went through a serious crisis starting with the bankruptcy of Lehman Brothers, a major financial services firm. I found myself in a deep financial crisis because the investments in the market dried up completely and I could not raise sufficient funds to finance my project. To hedge over this crisis and to fund my dream start-up, I took up a real- estate project in my hometown Shimoga in Karnataka State. I enjoyed working on this project because it solved my immediate financial problems as well as it provided me with some badly-needed entrepreneurial success that helped me gain confidence as a budding entrepreneur. I used to spend the whole day working on the real-estate project, exposed to all the vagaries of nature, which made me strong physically and later in the evening, I would open my recently-bought SONY laptop and work on putting together my software venture. I quickly started finding small success in both the activities.

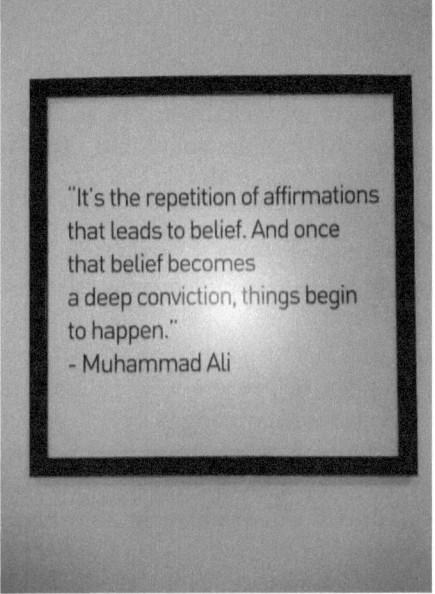

Inspiring words I found on the wall of a store in Bangalore

During this first phase of my entrepreneurial journey, the greatest learning was to convert fear into motivation. I learned to face the fear head-on, conquer it and move forward...on a daily basis.

Entrepreneurial Journey - Phase 2

To achieve success in building a good software company I needed to have the following;

- A good product idea
- Strong team dedicated people with complementary skill-sets
- An investor who would trust me and my dream

I had done the necessary homework while I was still working in Dubai and was on the lookout for an innovative product idea for my new start up. I use to read voraciously and did lot of groundwork and market research to identify something that was completely new; which I eventually found.

However, putting together a high-quality and dedicated team is extremely challenging. Two important things I had learned from reading books such as, 'High-Performance Entrepreneur' by Subroto Baghchi, Co-founder of Mind Tree Consulting and 'Simply Fly' by Captain Gopinath:

- To analyze and accept my own strengths and weaknesses
- Find people with complementary skills to fill the gaps

My stint at IIM Bangalore as a student of executive management program helped me a lot. During my IIMB days, I had connected with some amazing people, whose help I sought to identify and build a high-quality team members for my venture. I had also nurtured my association with two healthcare industry professionals in the US whom I had always dreamt of hiring as and when I was able to hire. I made a couple of trips to the US, and strengthened my association with them and made few new connections as well.

I was also helped in multiple ways by my engineering school buddies who have settled in USA. One of them, an outstanding Robotics Scientist joined us as our consulting data scientist and contributed immensely in developing and testing complicated predictive analytics algorithms for our software product. He continues to be my sounding board for all my current and future ventures.

Almost by chance, I found my mentor who has made a huge difference to my entrepreneurial life. A brilliant technical person from the semiconductor industry and an entrepreneur himself, he provided me the much-needed initial seed fund as well as the valuable hand-holding throughout my entrepreneurial journey. He has been my sounding board and a staunch supporter ever since.

One thing was certain. If I were to build a global venture, I needed to have a strong finance person in my core team. So I decided at the outset to find the right person who could take care of the finance aspect of running my business. I searched and waited for a very long time....almost two years. Finally, I found a young chartered accountant and an astute finance strategist. Both of us connected almost immediately and I made him my co-founder at Axiom. He took care of the finance department of the business. I know for certain, that had I not had the support of someone like him in that role, I would have committed expensive, irreversible mistakes. He helped me find the necessary investments and managed the corporate finance meticulously. While looking out for the finance person, I had already started to identify strong Technical hands for important functions like Product Management, CTO, Solution Architect, COO, Delivery head etc. Soon I found all the people.

One Oxford Centre in downtown Pittsburgh, location of Axiom HQ

This brings me to my personal belief and experience that entrepreneurship is an opportunity to go beyond oneself—financial goals, sales figures, ego satisfaction, sense of personal achievement. For me, it is a spiritual journey and experience. I met my spiritual Guru who taught me that, if your inner soul is satisfied and ratifies your intentions and actions, only then will you enjoy your entrepreneurship. If there is a disconnect then you may not be able to weather the vagaries of the journey.

Meanwhile, my software venture took off pretty well and we built a USA headquartered (in Pittsburgh PA) global organization with R&D Centre in Bangalore, India. Ours was a multi-cultural team comprising of Indians, Americans and people from other nationalities. We worked with some of the biggest names in US healthcare industry and also built an impressive partnership with world-renowned universities such as Carnegie Mellon University (CMU). Our teams in the USA and in India developed amazing solutions for complicated healthcare problems such as cancer treatment, population health, and clinical predictive data analytics.

Personally, I became a truly global entrepreneur and travelled extensively, met many interesting people, made lasting friendships and built enduring business relationships. The knowledge gained through my experience in building my venture has been extraordinary.

Traits for successful entrepreneurship

Entrepreneurial success is a slow and long journey. Patience and perseverance are the two important qualities for an entrepreneur. As I have said at the beginning, the journey is fraught with many ups and downs. Giving up is an easy choice. But you discover your strength of character in times of distress and failure.

The courage to explore unchartered territory is the hallmark of an entrepreneur. One has to be curious and adventurous enough. The story of Christopher Columbus has been my inspiration since my childhood. As a young boy, I was mesmerized with his story of courage and perseverance. I greatly admired Columbus for building a team of co-travelers and for convincing Queen Isabella to fund his voyage, which led to the discovery of the 'new' world. He risked everything for what he believed in. Aren't these qualities the mantra for entrepreneurial success?

Education – Geographies, People and Cultures

Traveling across geographies and interacting with different cultures provided me immense scope for personal and professional growth. Personal growth is possible only when you are a keen observer of human behavior and a constant learner. My own individuality started taking shape only when I found myself exposed to people from different walks of life, with a wide richness of compelling characters.

All through my student life, I have been in a state of constant flux. From early schooling in Marathi medium, which wasn't my mother tongue but had to study because my father worked in the Maharashtra State Government, to an abrupt change to a Kannada-medium (my mother tongue) school in Shimoga, where my grandparents lived. Then to a boarding school, where my emotional and physical health deteriorated; and finally to a school in the bordering town of Karnataka, about 20 km from where my parents lived in Maharashtra; that was a lot of churning for a lad between 12 to 15 years of age. This new school made a big difference to my perspective of life. I had to commute 20 km, all by myself every day in varying modes of transport; one day the public bus, another day as a hitchhiker on a truck or a lorry. I was exposed to a multi-cultural world – a Punjabi speaking driver one day, a Tamilian or a Telugu speaking driver another day. I suddenly became aware of a world outside of me. I picked up lingos from each of them; I was fascinated by their approach to life and work. These were simple people living uncomplicated lives, living small dreams. Life suddenly seemed beautiful and motivating.

Later I joined a reputed engineering college in Hubli in north Karnataka and that opened an entirely new and exciting world for me.

Engineering in Electronics and Communication was an obvious choice for two reasons:

- Computers and Electronics were the big buzz words of the time.
- I was fascinated and inspired by the use of artificial intelligence and robotics in Steven Spielberg and Star Wars movies that I never missed to watch.

I joined Electronics engineering much against my father's choice of Civil Engineering. Besides, I happened to be the first in my family to pursue Electronics Engineering. In a sense, by then I had already started thinking and doing things independently. The engineering course was a lot of hardship. We did not have faculty members for several subjects. I was very passionate and committed. I fought it out in my own style.

After engineering, my obvious professional option was to join a public sector unit such as BEL or BHEL. One incident changed my course. During the final year, an exhibition was organized as a platform for students to showcase their projects. A famous personality was invited to visit the exhibition. All my other team members backed out from making the presentation to the visiting dignitary. I was encouraged to do the presentation and I did it decently well. Our project won a prize too. My presentation skills were also appreciated. That is when I discovered that I probably would not be very happy being tied down to a computer desk in some remote corner of the organization. It was then that I discovered the sales and marketing persona in myself. That is when I decided to pursue a career in sales and marketing.

It took a while to get a good job in this profession. I joined corporate houses like Philips and enjoyed my stint there. After a decade in the industry, I did an executive management course at IIM, Bangalore.

During my days at engineering college and at IIMB I was exposed to some of the most brilliant minds. I learned tremendously from all my associations. I made sure I moved around with people who were experienced and knowledgeable. Such associations are a great way to learn and mold yourself. People have always been a great asset for me. IIMB was the most intellectually stimulating environment. I was exposed to the best of brains, best of practices, best of management studies and professors. IIMB was also the most wholesome multicultural environment. We were part of a community of students from all parts of India and from foreign shores. Learning is everywhere. Every interaction is a scope for learning. I believe that people are one of the best sources of knowledge.

Besides people, travel is the next best teacher. During my stint in Dubai, I traveled all over the Middle East and learned their work ethic and method, their way of running a business. In the USA, as I have traveled across that vast country, I learned a lot about the IT industry and about the vibrant startup culture. I had first-hand exposure to the entire process of starting up a business.

My journey continues....I have now founded a start-up incubation center called 'Let's START' where I am helping young entrepreneurs to build their start-ups by providing them a highly-stimulating work place and mentoring services. In a way I am living my entrepreneurial dream all over again.

My vision

I have been nurturing a dream inspired by my experience of the IIMB atmosphere and how it can enrich a person in more ways than one. I envision dedicating the next decade or so of my life to establishing a world-class university! This institution, I envision to be a cultural melting pot – to attract best brains from all over the world— with the purpose of solving problems through practical approaches. I intend to address teething problems in the following sectors – Environment, Agriculture, Healthcare, Civic Utilities, Education, and Public Sanitation. Education is my way of giving back to society, by empowering the youth of this nation.

SHASHIDHAR JAKKALI

Shashidhar Jakkali is a serial entrepreneur and a start-up mentor looking to discover future unicorns. After spending over a decade in corporate jobs in the global healthcare IT industry, he founded Pittsburgh PA USA headquartered healthcare data analytics firm, 'Axiom Health Intellect Systems' in 2008. Recently in 2016, he has co-founded business incubation &co-working company named 'Let's START' and a block chain technology based FinTech company named 'BlockEnable'. He is currently assisting over a dozen start-ups to grow their business globally. He is also personally mentoring and hand-holding two 'unicorns-in-the-making' start-ups to establish their business in the global markets.

Being not exactly from a businessman's family, Shashidhar had to work very hard sometimes against and sometimes around many challenges to become an entrepreneur. Having set high goals of becoming a global entrepreneur, he took a keen interest in understanding the cultural nuances in dynamically evolving multi-cultural societies such as India, USA, and UAE where people from geographically different locations come together to work coherently to achieve common objectives.

It is said the journey of thousand miles starts with the first step. Shashidhar has experienced this first hand and his amazing journey continues. During his global entrepreneurial journey, he has visited over a dozen countries, travelled extensively within those countries, interacted with cross-section of local population, tried his hands at local languages/customs & foods, made lasting friends with vast spectrum of people from various walks of life, encountered dangers & thrills, managed ultra-thin resources as well as luxuries, drove thousands of miles and snapped up over 10,000 interesting photographs.

On the business front; he has worked for corporates, founded technology companies, built a start-up incubation center, raised investments in India & abroad and has led teams of outstanding talent to develop globally competitive products and services.

As part of his life vision, his ambition is to set up a truly 'Global University' where experts from best of the institutions from different countries impart their wisdom and knowledge to solve the most pressing problems faced by societies worldwide.

Shashidhar lives in Bangalore India, with his wife Rekha, daughters Nidhi & Sharadhi and his extended family. His other passions include traveling, spiritual deep-dives and building utopian societies on thoughts based on 'universe is one family' concepts propagated by Swami Vivekananda and other great spiritual leaders.

Shashidhar can be contacted for inquiries related to start-ups mentoring, investments, global industry best practices, building multi-cultural teams and knowledge exchange programs with universities worldwide.

LinkedIn: http://linkedin.com/in/shashidhar-jakkali-93b4a42

2

GROUND ZERO

- BY PHIL BRITTEN, INTERNATIONAL SPEAKER, AUTHOR, ENTREPRENEUR & FOUNDER OF BUSINESS GROWTH

I was not born to be a businessman. None of us are in fact. We are all born with certain skills and talents yes, but often it's the world or society that begins to interpret what those skills and talents mean for our life path and direction.

I believe that being in business or making the decision to become an entrepreneur is a choice. Often not an easy choice as the odds are largely stacked against those brave enough to venture forwards. They are the ones who dig deep within, taking their natural skills and talents, taking stock of their weaknesses and the ones who decide to embrace their one shot at life.

They make a choice to become far more than what the world

may try to define them as, rather they take ownership of their world and create their own definition, their own legacy.

Growing up in Exmouth, in country Western Australia (WA), I lived a very carefree childhood. Full of long sunny days on the beach my life revolved around the outdoors. One of the most beautiful places on earth, with soft white sandy shores and turquoise waves, the town itself was removed from much of the hustle and bustle of a large city, yet it had everything I needed as a young boy growing up. I was very driven from a young age to become involved in professional sports and so the time came as a I grew up and entered into high school, that I needed to move closer to WA's capital city, Perth.

My teenage years were firmly focussed on my ambitions as an Australian Rules Footballer (AFL) and I was working hard to establish myself as an elite sportsman in this area. I found a significant level of success and my hard work for many years and dedication was finally starting to see everything come together. However, as I prepared to consolidate my career path along this road, my life was torn apart in a terrorist attack, a 700kg bomb detonated by terrorists 20 metres away from where I stood at the age of 22. Ground zero. All my plans for the future completely destroyed. To say I was lost would be an overwhelming understatement.

The skills and talents that I was born with was a competitive nature, an inquisitive soul and being naturally athletic. This is what had led me to believe I was destined to become a professional sportsman, a career that I had invested myself heavily into and embraced in the fullest. Until the moment of the terror attacks.

A moment, that made me reconsider every definition I had placed around myself until that very point.

And a moment that threatened to become my ultimate definition unless I dug deep within and searched for what it was that truly inspired, motivated and would ultimately define me by MY own choice

After the Bali bombing in 2002, I had been burnt to 60% of my body and my professional AFL career and ambitions, all but over. My trade, a refrigeration air-conditioning mechanic (because everyone tells you to have a good trade behind you in case things don't work out) wasn't working out so well for me as I could no longer physically take on this role either.

I had to make a choice. I still had my naturally born skills and talents but I no longer had the path I believed I was destined for in front of me. I decided to start doing what felt good, what felt right, for me, in my case, this was Martial Arts.

Piece by piece I began putting my life back together and it was through this process that I found my ultimate passion and purpose. I started spending more time in my passions, working on the speaking circuit as well as in martial arts and found that in these industries, I was in flow, working in areas that inspired me enough to get through the late nights, the sacrifices and the obstacles.

I began to diversify and one venture led to another, all stemming from a desire to help and serve others. It was along this path that I realised that by doing what truly fulfilled me, it gave me the fuel and drive I needed to turn my passions into a profit.

I've been building businesses and speaking professionally for the past 15 years. A keen student, not initially in a traditional sense, I immersed myself with mentors, networked and critically examined the world around me and its relationship to industry. I began to learn about business, every angle, every topic from the ground up. I started to look at how this would apply to me and the industry I wanted to navigate. Martial Arts was largely considered a hobby, a part-time side business, not necessarily a profitable venture.

Perhaps this was now my competitive nature coming into play, but I believed that this hobby, could become something more. By purchasing a small existing martial arts school and innovating both business development strategies and current industry models, revenue began to steadily increase on an average of 16% per annum and within 18 months, student numbers had increased by

46.7% and revenue 98.2%.

Over the next few years, one martial arts school expanded into three, by 2010 becoming one of the largest single-owned multiple school organisations in Australia and one of the most profitable in the world (the top 1% in Industry).

My portfolio of three martial arts school expanded into seven different business ventures; diversifying into defence, corporate services training, business consulting and public speaking.

Each business, in spite of being spread across various industries, has a common thread - they are created to provide opportunities for people to build themselves up and to better themselves.

Summit Success, based in Western Australia is the overarching Company I own which controls The WA Institute of Martial Arts (WAIMA), The Institute of Martial Arts (TIMA), International Defensive Solutions (IDS), Master Your Destiny (MYD) and WA Martial Arts Supplies.

From an employee in my industry, to operator, to business owner and now to investor, growth and change is a part of that journey. If you never change, you never grow and if you're unwilling to grow, very little will change.

I grew with my business model and expanded into not only being good at business and the businesses I owned but into an arena where I now teach others how to do that for themselves. In other words, I practice what I preach.

Marketing and sales is probably one of the largest industries to see a shift in its fundamental practices over the past 15 years. Despite having so much more access to customers than ever before and a greater international reach that a only generation ago, it would have seemed unimaginable, it takes 16 - 20 times for a person to be exposed to your brand before they make the decision to become a customer or client.

Standing out from the crowd, forward thinking and getting that competitive edge while remaining efficient in how you do all of that can make or break your business. You need to keep your brand front and centre where people's attention is the most, rather than trying to bring their attention over towards you.

With 100 people in a room all screaming 'look at me', you can join into that chorus with a 1 in 100 chance of success or you can step directly in front your potential client and get yourself a 50/50 chance. They'll either like your business or they won't but you're already in front because they'll now definitely have seen you.

For example, we all know people are consumed daily by social media, yet very few business owners know how to position their business front and centre in this arena, how to leverage off this mass marketing platform, other than setting up a simple page. A page, in millions of other pages.

People no longer want be sold to in a traditional sense; clients are market savvy, they are researched and can often see through fancy advertising campaigns. They want to be in control of their decisions to buy, decisions largely influenced by whether or not they think you will add value to their life. Decisions based upon trust and a personal connection with your brand. People want to do business with those that they know, like and trust. And you create that connection by providing consistent value, not just value to obtain that initial sale.

I live in Western Australia, where bushfires are a part of life, but what never ceases to amaze me when driving through an area previously ravaged by a fire, is the amount of new growth once the ashes have settled. Seeing adaptation come to life and regenerating the landscape stronger than ever before is awe inspiring.

The past 30 years of industry has seen a bushfire of its own, the flames of technology swept through traditional landscapes, burning down boundaries and removing traditional barriers of business. The opportunity for dynamic growth, for regeneration is there for those willing to adapt, innovate and rise up stronger than ever before out of the ashes.

My primary business is innovating, it's taking what people already have, what people already know and getting them to pull it completely apart and build it back together in a way that works best for them, not the other way around. I take people from where they are now and help get them to where they really want to be, not only in their professional lives, but their personal lives also.

I am known internationally for my ability to inspire, innovate and influence audiences on a personal level to get out there and be the very best that they can be. I teach people how to not only build and grow but also to monetise their business so that they can truly pursue what they love, rather than simply dreaming with the 'one day when' mindset.

I have worked on international stages alongside Andy Harrington - The World's #1 Public Speaking Expert, Gary Vaynerchuck (Investor and Serial Entrepreneur) and many more; consulted for clients including BHP, Roy Hill Mines, Red Cross in Australia, UK-based Elite Property Bootcamp and the US-based Educational Funding Company (EFC).

Being in business for yourself or being an entrepreneur is not something that can be done without passion. The more you invest into yourself and your vision, the more passionate you have to become and it's only natural that this translates into your personal life as well.

Successful entrepreneurs are passionate and motivated individuals and I am no different.

My professional passions, once I stripped down all the individual levels are very simple. It's helping take people from where they are to where they want to be. I do this by combining my skills as an inspirational and motivational speaker and my real-life experiences in building highly successful businesses. Challenging the status quo, I work with clients to become the change that they need and give them the skills and techniques required to find long-term and lasting success.

In my personal life, I'm a passionate adventurer. I believe you have one life and that life should be lived to the fullest. Travelling, immersing myself in breathtaking landscapes and diverse cultures inspires me to keep my own world in perspective and I love to do this with my family. Being able to guide my children's life experiences, seeing the world all over again through their eyes is what renews my soul. Being a father to my children is the greatest privilege on earth; it's important that no matter how hard you work and push for your passions on a professional level, that you keep your personal passions front and centre at all times.

When I'm not working, I'm at home with my family. In the garden, in the pool, at the park, the beach, spending time together just playing and having fun is my ultimate day off. I run a laptop lifestyle so it's important that I keep a very clear line between my downtime and my work time or things can begin to cross over. It would end up feeling as if you've never switched 'off' so I've learnt to make that line a defined one. The phone is off, the computer is away and I make sure that I'm completely present in whatever it is that I'm doing.

Giving back to society also makes up a big part of my life. As an Ambassador for The Adventurers, a unique Australian charity which is committed to finding a cure for Childhood Cancer, I have led adventures including a unique survival trek through the remote Kimberley region in WA, climbed Mt Kilimanjaro in Africa and Gran Paradiso in Italy and trekked the Kokoda Trail in Papua New Guinea. The Adventures raise much needed funds for childhood cancer research, millions of dollars per year, and has made such significant developments in the understanding of this disease.

I am also an Advisor for the Bali Peace Park Association which is working towards developing a Peace Park on the site of former Sari Club site, where one of the 2002 Bali bombings occurred. As survivor from those attacks, this project is very close to my heart. One of the greatest feelings in the world is that of being able to do good for others and I always encourage people to get involved with a charitable project that will have meaning for them.

I have been recognised with the WA Business News 40 Under

40 Awards, The Nifnex Influential 100, Momentum Forum Most Inspiring Man of the Year and Professional Speakers Academy (UK) Australian Speaker of the Year for the past two years.

In spite of all of this, and no matter how much I love what I do, the one thing that I would not compromise is the balance of spending time with my family. I don't live to work, I work to live and I want to make sure that I can be there for the important moments in their lives. I am committed to making memories with my loved ones and being a bystander in their lives is not part of that plan.

From ground zero, where my story almost ended, but instead became the point where my story truly began, I built myself and my businesses out of the ashes. I took everything that I knew and combined it with everything that I believed in and committed myself to growth.

My goal is that of legacy. I want to be remembered for being a leader in inspiring and teaching others to build, grow and monetise a business based on their passions, one that they can control, not that controls them.

Each of us has a different amount of time on this earth but we each only get one time. One chance to make the most of our gifts and to make a lasting contribution to our society. If everyone is able to make the most of those gifts and do so with purpose, it is my belief that our world will continue to become a much better place.

Phil Britten

Phil's unique successes found him a winner of the coveted wa business news '40under40' award in recognition as one of the top entrepreneurs. He was also awarded as a top four finalist for the award's highest accolade of 'first among equals'. That same year, he was named 'most inspiring man of the year' by momentum forum and more recently recognized as the professional speakers academy's 'Australian Speaker of the Year' as well as receiving a 'most influential 100' award by nifnex.

Now, after building six businesses from the ground up, phil has cemented his position as an international speaker, sharing his expertise, assisting both individuals and companies grow and monetize their business and life ambitions.

By also drawing on his unique real-life experience of triumph over tragedy with burns to 60% of his body following a terrorist bomb attack, Phil is able to connect with his audience on a personal level, driving home the importance of taking action now. A committed ambassador for charity with the telethon adventurers, Phil has raised both funds and awareness to find a cure for childhood cancer by climbing to the peaks of gran paradiso (the highest peak in the Italian alps) and mount Kilimanjaro (one of the seven summits), trekking both the Kokoda trail as well as a 7 day survival trek through the Australian outback.

From falling into one of the darkest moments his life had to offer, Phil's determination has seen his star rapidly rise once more. Faced with the choice between being a victim or a survivor, he instead redefined the model of 'do whatever it takes', and chose to become a warrior.

3

THE CONTRARIAN RULE – CONTRARIAN ALWAYS WIN!

- BY C T PARUN, FATHER OF CONTRA TRADING

Contrarianism is a whole philosophy. Contrarian thinking is nothing but doing things in unconventional ways; of shedding the skin of herd-mentality; of having a mind of your own; and the guts to stand by what you think is right.

I have been associated with the financial market, stock market, trading and investment business for the last two decades. Warren Buffett is my role model. He is a contrarian. Perhaps the greatest contrarian of our times. Over a period of 6 decades, he has amassed a gross wealth of 86 billion dollars because of his contrarian thinking. He says, "Be fearful when others are greedy and greedy when others are fearful." This is the hallmark of a contra investor. I have succeeded as a contra trader and the market has identified my success to the extent that most of them do not know me by my name, but know me only as a contra trader. They refer to me as CT. So I have added those initials to my name! I am

C T Parun!

I currently manage private syndicate funds, advise base metal trading organizations, NSE/NYSE members, consult for Wall Street and Dalal Street firms and help individuals, retail traders and investment communities.

I did not start off as a contrarian. I came into trading, like everyone else, with a traditional mindset. I traded like everyone else. And just as for everyone else, the market was not favorable to me. I was not rewarded by the market as expected. I could not quite figure out just yet, why small retail traders and investors could not make extreme gains. There was no consistency in the outcome for people like us.

Around the same time, I had the opportunity to work as a consultant for developing certain functional software systems that directly integrated to the major stock exchanges in real time. While implementing this project I had ample scope to analyze order flows in real time. I noticed that one particular trading community always made money all through the year irrespective of market conditions. The other community, the small trader always lost to those communities. I analyzed and probed further, to finally understand that there is one single most important factor that determines the outcome: the mindset of the trader. That is when I closely studied the entire financial trading ecosystem.

There are essentially just two types of mindsets: the traditional and the contrarian. The contrarian trader makes consistent profits all through the year, while the traditional trader loses most of the times. Contrarians typically go against the majority evaluation of a certain investment or a company's stock. When the majority decides not to invest, a contrarian seeks to invest, and vice versa. Because, majority perception itself, either overvalues or undervalues the profit and loss potential. So I began to perceive the entire business of financial transactions in trading from a contrarian point of view. And it worked. I started making consistent profits all through the year. I was riding high on the investment wave.

Contrarianism for a purpose

One incident added a different dimension to what I was doing. It a very humane purpose to my profession. I happened to meet a gentleman named Mohan. He looked very sickly, frail and emaciated. His skin was dappled with lesions. It seemed like he was afflicted with cancer. I very gently probed to understand his health condition. I was appalled to discover that his condition was an occupational hazard. He worked in the laboratory of a chemical organization, heating chemicals. He was constantly ingesting chemical fumes. He was provided masks which were designed for a single day use. But due to cost cutting, they were forced to wear the same mask for a week! I said why not look for a job change. He said that his profile and experience would fetch him only a similar job, irrespective of the company. And then, quite without thinking, I said, "Quit your job. Nothing is more important than health." He was furious. He asked me, "Who will support my family? Who will feed them?" He laughed condescendingly and walked away.

I felt ashamed. I was disturbed. I met him again and asked him if he was willing to quit his job if I showed him a way to earn money. His salary was about twenty-eight thousand rupees. I said I could show him how to earn up to sixty thousand a month. I sat him down and explained the art and science of financial trading. I arranged a small trading capital for him so he could begin trading and start making money from the market. He started and in a few months generated consistent profits month on month. Shortly, he quit his profession as well and completely recovered his health.

Knowledge and Skill Transfer

This experience compelled me to create small traders out of the labor community, which was being grossly exploited by employers in India and abroad. Today, I perceive this as an opportunity to help, as spiritual wealth is more valuable than financial wealth. Now it has become my sole purpose to enable the huge community of small traders with the knowledge and skill to become contrarian traders. The larger companies and trading houses are adept at contrarian trading. The method of contrarian trading itself was kept a secret all these decades. Hence, the rich became richer and the poor became poorer. I want to decentralize wealth. Wealth must get distributed to the economically poor sections of the society. As a thought leader in the domain of contra trading, my mission is to spread awareness and convert more and more common people into contrarians so they can benefit from the financial trading market.

I have developed a 6-month course module of seven contra capsules for skill and knowledge transfer. Skill transfer is a step-by-step, experiential and system-oriented process. I have simplified and decoded the contra-trading principle and it can be applied to any account size ranging from 100 dollars to a million dollars.

The greatest challenge is to change the mindset of people who come for training. We first neutralize their mindset, because most of them are afflicted with herd mentality -- do what the majority does; go where most go. Then we instill the contrarian mindset in them. I offer one-on-one consultation, group coaching and seminars.

A one-on-one is typically private coaching and requires mutual trust. I understand the client's background, financial status etc. and chart out a unique roadmap to achieve his financial goals. Group coaching is typically a small group of 6-8 people who could be a group of relatives, friends or colleagues, say, doctors, etc. Finally, the seminar-based model is more a generic kind of coaching where the public is invited.

Anatomy of the Financial Market

From my experience and understanding, I believe that there are three pillars for exponential financial growth of any Individual: Business, Financial Market and Real Estate, and the three types of social status derived on these three pillars are: Survivors, Performers and Excellence.

Survivors are typically those who are not associated with any one of these pillars that include working communities, self-employed professionals such as doctors, advocates, insurance agents, small farmers, small shop owners etc. They are always scarce of money and they trade their time for money.

Performers are those who are associated with any one of these pillars either business or real-estate. They have some money, not big money.

Excellence are those who are associated with all the three pillars. They have abundance of money. E.g. Azim Premji, Narayan Murthy and so on. They are in Business, Financial Market and Real-estate.

Why Performers Cannot Make Big Money

Performers typically save their money in fixed deposits and mutual funds. For instance, for a deposit of 1 lakh, you earn an interest of approximately 8%. The recorded global inflation is about 12%; unrecorded is much more. That means, you received +8% from the bank and inflation is -11%. In net, your investment is eroded by -3% at the end of the year. Suppose you keep your money in fixed deposit for a 10 year period, your capital is eroded by over 50%. So saving in this manner is slow poison.

The one quality required to succeed in the financial trading market is an open mind to adapt to contrarian thinking. No educational qualification, work experience, IQ level works in this business. You only have to imbibe the contrarian approach. Acquiring wealth is easy. But retaining and multiplying wealth is very difficult. The only way is to cultivate a contrarian mindset.

I want to catalyze and change the lives of common people so they can achieve their financial goals and enhance social mobility. I am looking at creating mass social mobility in India through creating mass literacy and awareness of the financial market. This will, in turn, create consistent profits, stress-less profits, capital and investment multiplication and profit amplification.

C T Parun

EXPERT ON

- Wealth Building
- Leadership
- Innovation
- Performance Improvement
- Business Profit Growth

ABOUT CT PARUN

- Thought leader in the area of Contra Trading & Investments

- CT Parun decoded the formulas to make consistent Profits from various markets.

- Over 20 years of experience in Financial Market, Stock Market Trading & Investments.

- CT Parun as a catalyst is helping and guided a lot of people to change their life and achieve their financial goals.

- CT Parun has vast experience of trading in the global markets. He had been associated with large institutions in the past and now spends his time managing private syndicate funds, advising base metal trading organisations, NSE/NYSE Members, Consulting Wall Street and Dalal Street Firms and helping out Individuals(HNI) and Retail Traders &Investment communities.

- Inventor of Contra Volume, Contra Insider which is being widely used by large institutions to generate profits.

- CT Parun's famous quote says

"CONTRARIAN DO WHAT AVERAGE CROWD DOES NOT DO CONTRARIAN DO NOT DO WHAT AVERAGE CROWD DOES"

4

ARE THE MESSENGER WHO TRANSFORMS LIVES

- BY DR. JOANNE MESSENGER, DRJO IS A TRUE AMBASSADOR FOR HEALING: CHIROPRACTOR AUTHOR (BEINONEPEACE, HOWTOBALANCEYOURHORMONES) RETREATS

I looked around at the "be rich and famous at all costs" worlds of business, healing and spiritual development... and felt frustrated at the numbers of people either spinning their wheels getting nowhere fulfilling, or with lots to offer yet were jaded, burned out and not as financially independent as they'd hoped.

I'm Dr Joanne Messenger. My friends call me "Dr Jo" or "Jo".

I am a messenger and I am in the business of transforming lives.

I have a flair for seeing people's gifts and potentials, what blocks them, and how to resolve their mismatch.

I am known for my authenticity, heart, understanding people's predicaments, and knowing what to do about it.

I have a knack for hearing higher guidance and translating it into practical, fulfilling and profitable solutions with a no-drama approach.

I love inspiring people to live the life they were born for with less fear and more peace.

In a world where stress over money, relationships, health and time dominate, I decided to defy the trend.

I knew people didn't have to be born with a healing gift to heal themselves, a business gift to thrive in their community, clairvoyant gifts to follow their intuition, or social media know-how to have the relationships of their dreams.

Like many people just like you, I know what it's like to start on a shoestring budget with a vague idea, rather than a crystal-clear plan… the nerve-racking fear of never feeling quite ready… and the desire for things to happen much faster and safer than what life had offered so far…

Even so, I didn't wait for everything to be perfect. I knew in my heart that excellent was okay. Now I help people heal their hearts, minds, bodies, businesses and relationships… lifting them into alignment with what "they were born for" rather than settling for less.

"Dr. Joanne "Jo" Messenger has been listed as one of Adyar's Great Australian Authors. She's written Be in One Peace, How to Balance Your Hormones, and has over 35 years experience as a chiropractor, Chiron Healer, course facilitator and public speaker."

"With Dr Messenger you'll find an affinity with her easy conversational style and professional persona. You'll feel she's talking to you personally, guiding you on an important path that will ultimately lead to both physical healing and fulfilment of your divine plan".

EARLY BEGINNINGS

I grew up in country Western Australia as the youngest of seven children. With six older brothers to compete with, it's natural I became a high achiever. I was School Captain, Dux of School, Highest Citizenship and Sports Achiever. One year, I even won high jump which is extraordinary for my height.

I was third in the state for competition gymnastics by the time I was ten years old. However, when I was twelve I fractured my pelvis in a trampoline fall with major implications for my health. Within a year my hormonal cycle stopped, I had my appendix removed, and my entire alignment shifted.

This experience forced me to learn everything I could about healing, nutrition, energy and the divine plan.

At seventeen, I moved to Melbourne on the other side of Australia without knowing anybody at all, to study chiropractic which I later followed with nutrition, energy healing, yoga, meditation, herbs, essential oils and whatever I could soak up. I wanted to know everything I could about healing myself which then became what I used to help heal others. I became the principal of the Chiron Healing school and taught all the teachers.

Now a health care professional, I share my lifelong quest for healing, releasing karma and living your life purpose – with less fear and more peace.

I currently live just north of Sydney, by the ocean I love. I'm committed to enhancing my own health and living a sustainable lifestyle as much as possible. I eat what suits my body best, and exercise and meditate most days. The healthier, happier and more fulfilled I am, the more I can help others to find their best path forward.

I work with people on all levels with their health, businesses, relationships and life direction, helping them move forward by using step-by-step skills and techniques that are based on practical experience.

I know what it's like to want to feel better, and how frustrating that dream can be to attain. The good news is I've gathered all the best tools and techniques through practical experience plus studying the science and methods, that are essential to help people just like you, to get back on track.

My foundation exercises are running, walking, swimming, and yoga. Most of my days start with exercise then meditation.
I like to start work a little later so I can complete my own rituals and self-care first. My experience is, if I leave my exercise until the end of the day, it doesn't happen. "Do wat works is my philosophy".

My work day offers something for everyone. It varies between:
One to one patients: Skype of face-to-face using chiropractic, energy healing, nutrition et al to help people resolve their aches, disease, emotional pains and raise their health and wellness.

Writing: I've written two self-help books (Be in One Peace and How to Balance Your Hormones) and thin I've got another ten or so, in me waiting to take form.

Programs, Workshops and Retreats: To help people on their healing journey and how to live their life purpose with fulfilment as effortlessly as possible.

Blogging: Social media is a quick and easy way to say something useful, succinctly.

Meditating: I include meditation in my work day as well as my personal rituals. If you're not aligned with your higher self and purpose your business will be a struggle as well as your health and relationships.

Updating Websites: Never ending! jomessenger.com, drjoannemessenger.com

I'm passionate about helping people who want to make a difference in the world yet get stuck and struggle with their self-esteem, confidence, health, money, time, knowing what steps to take, and need support along the way.

I help them get clear, remove their blocks, and live their purpose for a profit, without turning their life upside down.

PROFESSIONAL PERSONA

I'm generally an organised person who likes to run on time. Every now and then I'll lapse into not committing to anything until ten minutes before (at best).

"Dr Jo's natural professional style and concise instructions make understanding her ideas and putting them into practice effortless. Her voice is strong and authoritative, giving credibility to her assertions and directions. She is well organized and clearly demonstrates she is an experienced and knowledgeable author. Dr Jo presents her information with a natural flow and pacing that make her courses and books an easy "read", yet very useful and appreciated by her audience".

ACADEMIC MOJO

Dr Jo's academic qualifications are impressive. She has a Bachelor Degree in Applied Science (1982); a Diploma from the National Board of Chiropractic Examiners (USA); an Excellence Award in Radiology; a Diploma of Sacro-Occipital Technique; Practitioner and Teacher Certificates in Chiron Healing; Certificate IV in Assessment and Workplace Training; is a certified Yoga (RYTA200) teacher; is certified in Neuro Linguistic Programming (NLP) as applied to education; as well as studying Aromatherapy; Australian Bush Flower Essences; Essences of the Ancient Civilizations; Pleiadean Light Work and Pranic Healing

She has also been Principal of the Australian Energy School of Chiron & Vice President of the International Assoc of Chiron Healers. Inc., Treasurer of S.O.TO. A/Asia Ltd

Dr Jo helps people just like you, to reach their highest potential without turning their life upside down.

In a world where stress over money, health, relationships and time dominate, Dr Jo Messenger has defied the trend. She knows you don't have to be born rich to get wealthy, or have a healing gift to restore health or have the relationship of your dreams.

Like you, she knows what it's like to have a vague idea rather than a crystal clear plan... the fear of never feeling quite ready... and the desire for things to happen much faster and safer than they've been so far.

Dr Jo didn't wait for everything to be perfect, she knew in her heart that excellent was okay. She's authored two books and co-authored a third, taught courses internationally, and been in private practice for 35 years.

Dr Jo is just the person to help lift you into alignment with your true self and what you're born for, rather than settling for less.

Professional Persona

Dr Jo's natural and professional style and concise instructions make understanding her ideas and putting them into practice effortless. Her voice is strong and authoritative, giving credibility to her assertions and directions. Her writing and courses are well organized and clearly demonstrate she is an experienced and knowledgeable author and presenter. Dr Jo presents her information with a natural flow and pace that are very useful and appreciated by her audiences.

- Dr Jo has always been a high achiever:
- Early Highlights:
- Third in the state for gymnastics by age 10.
- School captain.
- Honours awards in academic excellence.
- Dux of school.
- Citizenship award.
- Accepted into the Melbourne chiropractic college at only 17yrs and graduated top of the class.

Real Qualifications:

- Bachelor Degree in Applied Science Chiropractic (1982)
- Diploma of National Board of Chiropractic Examiners (USA)
- Excellence Award in Radiology
- Diploma of Sacro-Occipital Technique
- Certified Yoga Teacher (RYTA200)
- Certified in Neuro Linguistic Programming (NLP) as

applied to education
- Level 3 Practitioner and teacher certificates in Chiron Healing
- Studied Aromatherapy; Australian Bush Flower Essences; Essences of the Ancient Civilizations; Pleiadean Light Work and Pranic Healing

Experience Worth a Mention:

- Published Be in One Peace
- Published How to Balance Your Hormones
- A Blog that's growing faster than a teenage boy on steroids
- Hosted my own weekly radio program on Highlands FM.
- Regular guest on the Coffee Break TV program
- Past treasurer of S.O.T.O. A/Asia Ltd,
- Founder and teacher of Blueprint Healing.
- Past Principal of the Australian Energy School of Chiron (AESC).
- Past Vice President of the International Association of Chiron Healers Inc.
- Taught the philosophies and techniques of energy and healing internationally.
- Guest speaker at International Flower Essence Conference.
- Guest speaker for Women at Work.
- Co-founder of Women for Women Australia

What Do Other People Say?

"About 12 months ago my life was in chaos.

After 23 years living interstate in Victoria I made the decision with my then husband to return to Central Coast NSW and share a house with my daughter and grand-daughter. Within a month my husband and I had separated and my life and both physical and mental health was in tatters. At this time a friend suggested I should see Dr Joanne Messenger, a chiropractor and Chiron Healer.

I did not know what to expect. But when I arrived for my first appointment I met a beautiful woman, with common-sense and compassion shining from within.

Initially I was seeing Joanne fortnightly and as she worked on repairing my "life blue print" I felt myself moving out of the state of fearfulness and terror that stopped me thinking and moving forward. I regained my sense of self and began re-connecting with my higher self and guides. I was no longer lost and alone. My general health improved. I shed kilos of weight with which I had protected myself and my blood pressure stabilised for the first time in years.

My visits are now monthly. For the first time in my life I greet each day with joy and a zest for life knowing that no matter what awaits me I have the tools I need to deal with it and move forward.
Life is a wonderful journey I have rediscovered! Thank you Joanne".

Annette

I have been a client of Joanne's for about 4 years and have found her Chiron Healing treatments to be soothing, gentle and often illuminating. Joanne is a gifted woman who has great intuition and understanding of people, situations and diagnoses.

Being in a room with Guardian Angels, Ascended Masters - surrounded and infused with God Energy and Love is sometimes overwhelming, invariably healing and more often than not, pretty much WOW!

More recently I've had the opportunity to learn with Joanne as a student in her 'Be in One Peace' seminar. I found these days informative, interesting and inspiring.

Her teaching style is encouraging and nurtures self discovery. I felt great benefits within the group sessions and many of the tips & techniques I use in an ongoing basis.

There is a lot on offer here and I would encourage anyone to see what they could get from a visit to Joanne. Thank-you.

Dr. Joanne Messenger

Dr. Joanne Messenger has been listed as one of Adyar's Great Australian Authors, is the author of Be in One Peace, a chiropractor, and has over 30 years experience as a course facilitator and public speaker.

When Dr Jo was twelve, she fractured her pelvis in a trampoline fall. The experience inspired in the young woman a desire to learn everything she could about healing, balance and energy.

Now a health care professional, she shares her lifelong quest for healing in How to Balance Your Hormones.

She knows what it's like to want to feel better, and how frustrating that dream can be to attain. The good news is she's gathered all the BEST TOOLS and techniques that are essential to get you back on track.

Using her techniques, you can live the life of your dreams, free from delinquent hormones, mood swings, and aberrant energy levels.

- Are you a hindrance to yourself?
- Do your moods and weight fluctuate?
- Are you eating your savings in chocolate or carbs?
- Have you lost your focus?
- Are you uncertain how you're going to feel when you wake in the morning?

If you don't sort this out now imagine what your life is going to be like in ten years!

5

DETOX AND DE-STRESS THROUGH LAUGHTER - THE STORY OF HASOVAN

- BY SAVITHA HOSMANE, FOUNDER, DIRECTOR AT HASOVAN PVT LTD

"Be compassionate towards self to become healthy, whole and vibrantly integrated."

Mindful-Wellbeing is at the crux of Hasovan; the driving philosophy. Haso in Hindi means to laugh and van in Sanskrit means grove--my organization is a 'laughing grove'--a grove where you can discover joy, happiness and the innate child in you. Our mission is to bring out the fountain of laughter from the deepest recesses of your being. After all, joy is an intrinsic feeling; an elemental emotion. Babies are joyful for no reason. That is a state of bliss: when happiness is a way of life, a state of existence, where we do not have to look for reasons to be happy.

Although an Instrumentation Engineer by qualification, I am now a Joy Engineer by choice. The monotony of working in a 9 to 5 job was already taking a toll on me, not to mention the stress. I was hunting for a job desperately and a friend suggested I turn to entrepreneurship. I liked the suggestion. However, I had no business idea and absolutely no money. However, the thought of entrepreneurship remained. My thoughts reclaimed a creative piece I had written some time ago, where I had expressed my innate quest for joy, happiness, health and laughter. I had envisioned, as a figment of imagination, treating people with doses of laughter. I wanted to make people happier, but solving their problems as an outsider was not my idea. Therefore, I decided to create a space entirely dedicated to laughter, whereby an individual can initiate the process of self-healing.

From this thought, was born the idea of creating a business opportunity that worked at reducing stress levels through laughter clinics. I thought of fancy names for my enterprise such as Laughter Paradise and Laughter Shangri La. I could not connect with these names, though. The search was on. Early one morning I started meditating as usual and the name Hasovan flashed out of nowhere. I connected with this name instantly. My friends and kin loved the name when they heard it. It upheld one of the important criterions of promoting and highlighting the wit and wisdom inherent in Indian culture to the world.

All I wanted to do was share happiness, joy and laughter, as I was and am a very fun loving person. I certified as a facilitator on Laughter Meditative Therapies from Osho Institute of Meditative therapies and a Laughter Leader from World Laughter Tour Inc., Ohio, USA. Thus in 2012, was born Hasovan, with a vision to spread happiness and reduce stress. It is perhaps the only startup dedicated entirely to enhance emotional wellness and mental wellbeing. The activities of Hasovan are entirely research-based and unearth mindful well-being, incorporating the tools of laughter, active meditation and awareness to strengthen the inner being.

The Mind Body Nexus

All of us are aware of the inextricable relationship between mind and body. The state of the body is a direct reflection of the state of mind. Migraines, ulcers, skin rashes (eczema), insomnia (inability to sleep well) are the body's way of indicating that the mind is unable to handle the stress it is being subjected to. Eating habits are a clear indication of the state of mind. Under duress, you will notice that your eating habits change. Either, you eat too less or too much. You begin to crave for salty, oily, sweet foods, which are artificial mood enhancers, although temporary and unhealthy options. Your bowel movements are affected. Constipation is, in fact, a disease of the mind. A mind that is unwilling to let go of issues has its impact on the body too. As the mind relaxes, the body relaxes too.

I experienced a classic case of psychosomatic disorder at a very young age. Rashes erupted on my limbs all of a sudden with excessive itching when I was 11 years old. I was on allopathic medication for a very long time. Topical application of ointments supplemented by oral medication is the general allopathic prescription. But years passed with no result. Allopathy focuses only on reducing or suppressing symptoms. It does not investigate the root cause of the problem or disease. I shifted to Ayurveda to no avail. The condition continued to adulthood. I realized that until I cleared my mind of all toxins, the skin condition would remain. I worked on addressing my stress triggers one by one and learned to manage my stress through laughter and happiness therapy and meditation. This was a process of self-exploration as I went deeper within myself. This real life exploration is what I have documented in the book, "Erupt with Joy". I could see the emotional baggage, which I had bottled up, from many years and the resultant turmoil. This was creating havoc on my health. The entire focus was to clear the inner anguish and active meditation was the path I chose. The results were amazing. It was only about 4 years ago, that I got rid of the skin condition that I had suffered for 3 decades. I was convinced that laughter and meditation are a means to alleviate stress, induced by various triggers.

Another experience strengthened my belief and gave direction towards embracing a practical approach to addressing real-life problems. A good friend was going through a divorce. She was shattered. Her morale and self-esteem were at an all-time low. She was under tremendous emotional trauma. While conducting therapy I realized that most of the times, life situations cannot be altered. What we can alter in such circumstances, is one's own perception of the situation and one's response to it. My friend was guilty, badgering herself for her failure to sustain the relationship. She had begun to hate herself. After a few sessions with me, she understood that life had to go on with or without a spouse. She accepted her situation and learned to move on. We realized in the process that as we unburden ourselves and let go of our pain, guilt, anger, hurt etc. we experience joy from within. It was one of the most miraculous experiences of my life. This was the message which I felt was to be shared with the world and it inspired me to devise and facilitate joyful workshops.

In the process, I also understood that addressing an emotional problem directly, was not a very productive method. As soon as you say that there is an emotional issue, the person becomes touchy and reluctant. In the Indian society, a lot of stigma is associated with emotional therapy. Therefore, we devised ways and methods to address such issues obliquely. The best method was through laughter, playfulness and fun as a means of identifying and addressing problems within oneself and of letting go, of venting out all that is stacked up in the mind.

Laughter Therapy

Medical research on laughter began only a couple of decades ago (mainly in the US and Europe), but it has produced evidence enough to consider it as an effective medical therapy. Research focuses on the correlation between emotions with specific parts of the body. Anger has negative effects on the heart and circulation system; stress on skin and stomach. Simultaneously, laughter has beneficial effects on immunity, pain tolerance, blood pressure, longevity, and illness symptoms. (Bennet & Lengacher, Mora Ripoll).

It is well-known that the mind has powerful effects on the body. Consequently, if we induce ourselves to positive thinking, we can be our best healers. The problem is that influencing our minds is not as easy. Some people consider themselves happy just because they suppress their anger, but this just prolongs and increases the pain.

Besides, laughter requires intelligence – to laugh, you require presence of mind, the ability to connect diverse ideas, a creative mind. It is not a question of analysis; it is a question of insight. Laughter is one of the natural mechanisms of releasing our trapped emotions, tensions, worries, stresses -- in short -- our entire negative emotional baggage that is suppressed and repressed. Most often, when we are in pain, we seek attention, pity, sympathy, which only helps in further fortifying the pain.

Scientific research has proved that laughter does more than just brightening up your day. Sharing a good laugh can improve your health significantly. The energy generated through laughter is potent enough to relieve us of negativity.

Health Benefits of Laughter

The entire focus is on laughter wellness as a lifestyle mantra and harnessing the power of laughter to promote health and wellbeing.

Strengthens your immune system – Laughter improves the body's natural defense mechanism by increasing the amount of immunoglobulins and antibody producing T cells in the body.

Laughter uplifts mood and body - Tiring day? Feeling Exhausted? A laugh can provide you with a full-body wake-up call leaving you energized and refreshed. Laughter also boosts oxygen intake and releases endorphins, the feel-good hormones that make you cheerful.

Protects your heart - Regular laughter is like getting a gym membership for your heart. It is known to lower blood pressure. Laughter is a great cardio workout. It improves the function of blood vessels and increases blood flow, which can help protect you against a heart attack and other cardiovascular problems.

Amazing Stress Buster - Our fast-paced life can significantly increase the levels of cortisol in our body, causing disorders such as stress, depression and anxiety. Laughter reduces the level of stress-inducing hormones and simultaneously reduces anxiety and stress that impact your body.

Best Weight Loss Buddy - Laughter can give you a full body workout as it raises your heart rate and caloric expenditure, resulting in about 10-40 calories burned over 15 minutes of laughter according to a recent study. Laughing tones your abs, as a good belly laugh exercises the diaphragm and contracts the abs.

With so much power to heal and renew, the ability to laugh easily and frequently is a tremendous shield against surmounting problems. Laughter is the sweetest medicine available for your body and mind; it enhances your relationships and supports both physical and emotional health.

Products and Services

Our whole therapeutic approach is built around these three elements.

- Founding philosophies = Mantras,
- Workshops and Techniques = Tantras
- Products = Yantras

Mantras

At Hasovan, we conduct niche wellness workshops, which are experiential in nature and designed to spread awareness about the importance of mindful well-being, by focusing on three main mantras:

- Laugh at Yourself
- Love Yourself
- Live Moment to Moment

Activities at Hasovan

- enhance flexible creative decision-making;
- improve focus and help attain work-life balance;
- help connect and communicate with self;
- aid us with coping strategies to manage everyday stress

The entire focus is to keep the therapeutic process light-hearted and playful with helpful techniques for inner health and positive relationships.

Tantras

Tantras are therapies or techniques that help de-clutter the mind and relax it completely.

Hasovan has carved niche experiential Lifestyle Management workshops. The workshop offerings are:

Exploring Joy within - A journey to attain inner harmony (2 hours to 1 day)

Explore and experience yourself in this session where we create opportunities to know the self. Understanding oneself helps in understanding others and this will strengthen team bonding. When people feel good, they are at their productive best.

Upbeat moods, research attests, encourage people view others and situations in a positive light. That, in turn enhances creativity and decision-making skills and predisposes people to be helpful.

Studies have shown that when a person experiences inner happiness, creativity, productivity, concentration and focus increases. People become more innovative in work and create a healthy balance at work and home.

After the completion of the introductory 'Exploring Joy Within' workshop, you can move on to advanced therapies called 'Reclaiming Your Inner Child' and 'Mystic Rose Therapy'.

These are advanced meditative therapies proposed and explained during workshops to relax the mind and add joy.

Reclaiming Inner Child - A seven-day workshop to become more playful.

We go deep inside and free-up conditioned and repressed energies and reconnect with our own inner child in this playful yet powerful therapy.

Once you regain the deep sense of innocence and happiness, it is possible to bring that playful quality into your everyday life and live with childlike vitality and joy.

Mystic Rose therapy

Mystic Rose is a three-week therapy of three hours a day. In the first week, through laughter, participants dissolve blocks of conditioning that smother their inner spontaneity and joy. This helps to remove inhibitions and repressions and creates new spaces within.

In the second week, suppressed sadness, that destroys joy, grace and beauty is expressed and released through tears. This is a detox process and unburdens agony so that one regains childlike innocence.

During the third week, the participant sits silently, just watching, listening and being sensitive. This process is not for beginners and only for advanced level participants.

People can enhance the quality of their lives by bringing about three attitudinal changes:

- Adopt a non-serious approach to life and to one's self. Take your work seriously, but not yourself.

- Adopt playfulness. Playfulness is joy manifested.

- Cleanse the mind through Unwinding Technique. When you go to bed, in your mind recreate the happenings of the day in reverse order, from the most recent to the first at daybreak. Your mind is taken slowly through all the stress and tension of the day, to the early-morning moment when you woke up and you were completely rested, stress-free, fresh and full of energy. When your mind reaches that state, you are automatically relaxed.

Turning the mind inward and introspecting can give an

indication of the state of mind.

Yantras

We are building innovative bio-medical relaxation inducing devices to support our activities. In the first phase, we are rolling out the Laughing chair and the Laughter Quotient App.

Laughing Chair is an intelligent seating arrangement, scientifically designed to relieve stress and improve health and holistic well-being of a person through laughter. This adjustable chair stimulates the various laugh points in our body at regular intervals. The chair in the final form plans to work with the three major senses - touch, hearing and sight - to simulate laughter. The functional prototype of the Laughing Chair is ready and patent pending.

Laughter Quotient is an Android-based application that helps determine the laughter quotient of a person.

Though we developed the products as functional prototypes with a lot of passion and dedication, we were not able to package it as a ready-to-use product for the market. Nevertheless, the concept attracted a lot of interest and curiosity and found creative expression in a short movie. The YouTube link to the movie is https://www.youtube.com/watch?v=a3ycT0D_DVo

The forthcoming products are in stealth mode. We are conducting extensive market survey to understand customer need and acceptance.

Forthcoming Book - Erupt with Joy

A journey of self-exploration to attain inner harmony in work and life. Erupt with Joy is a journey towards becoming emotionally and mindfully wise.

IN THESE PAGES, YOU WILL UNCOVER . . .

- The connection between the mind and body and its impact on health and well-being.

- That our actions are governed by our thoughts, emotions, feelings and moods.

- How to make conscious decision to play the game of life in a light-hearted manner.

Futuristic Goals

Hasovan intends to collaborate with various research-oriented technologists and doctors to develop more technological products beneficial to human relaxation.

Hasovan intends to go global and spread the joy concepts to every nook and corner of the world after the successful inception in India.

We intent to establish Hasovan Online School to spread benefits of being joyful globally.

The strategy is to rollout the concepts in various phases.

So far, I have been funding my venture with personal savings and from proceeds of the wellness programs, I have been conducting. We are looking at taking Hasovan to the next level. We have collaborated in India and abroad with associations such as the Osho Institute of Meditative Therapies and Steve Wilson & Co to diversify our activities and to expand our reach. So far, a few thousand people have undergone the wellness therapies; 200 have used the Laughter Quotient app; and 50 the Laughing Chair. Feedback from all of them has been very encouraging. We are collaborating with people with the right skills to develop more products and devices.

Follow us
https://www.facebook.com/pages/Hasovan/397872023573316
https://twitter.com/HasovanPvt
https://www.youtube.com/watch?v=a3ycT0D_DVo
Skype id: savithahosamane
https://in.linkedin.com/in/hosamane-savitha-0bb70a12

Savitha Hosamane

Savitha Hosamane is an entrepreneur, author and is on a mission to empower the inner being joyfully for attaining work-life harmony. An instrumentation engineer by qualification and now a Joyful engineer by choice chose to walk the path less travelled of unconventional business. Currently conducting workshops about the impact of Lifestyle diseases in the young population and equip them with skills to lead a harmonious and healthy life. Successfully impacted few thousands of people and is growing by the day. What began as creating innovative products for people to unburden themselves and release the stress has grown into a lifelong crusade of enabling people with self-explorative techniques/skills for managing their Lifestyles.

Was awarded patent-incentive by KCTU, Government of Karnataka for the first functional prototype of Laughing chair-an intelligent seating arrangement to relieve stress. Her venture Hasovan was chosen as a creative start-up and was awarded by being showcased in a short-movie. Also chosen among top 25 start-ups of India from AIMS-Smart city. Got featured in the book "Turning Points" of Uncommon people as one among 14 true life stories.

Follow us
https://www.facebook.com/pages/Hasovan/397872023573316
https://twitter.com/HasovanPvt
https://www.youtube.com/watch?v=a3ycT0D_DVo
Skype id: savithahosamane
https://in.linkedin.com/in/hosamane-savitha-0bb70a12

SHASHIDHAR JAKKALI

6

ARCHITECTING HEALTHY FAMILIES

- BY SUNITAA, CERTIFIED PARENT COACH, PARENTING EDUCATOR , VOICE COACH

After a while, I felt that if this knowledge is helping my family and others, then why not share and coach people on these techniques to enhance their quality of life. That is when I started a systematic, tailored workshop for small groups of mothers. But then again, each family had different issues. There were many variables, so much so that, a fixed approach or set of solutions would not work for all families. I began to customize workshops to suit the challenges and requirements of each family.

Fundamentally, I devise my workshops on a few principles.

1. Each family is different; the dynamics, the needs, the issues and challenges are different. As husband and wife, we come with set habits, idiosyncrasies, beliefs, prejudices and biases. All these are reflected in our social interactions

and personal development.

2. With so many variables, you obviously cannot have a fixed workshop for every family. The structure and the content must be customized. Of course, some broad principles may be applicable generically.

3. I don't judge parents or children. There are no good or bad parents or children. There are only effective and ineffective parents. Awareness and empathy are the keys to effective parenting and interpersonal relationships.

4. Behavior is only a manifestation of the mental and emotional landscape.

I do not want to label my job as an enterprise or business. It is more of a service; it gives me tremendous joy to share my knowledge and experience with the community of parents and children. Institutionalizing and commercializing it is not how I want to operate. I would rather work at my convenience and make each interaction meaningful and result-oriented. I am driven by my commitment to make the journey of parenting and growing up, a joyful and exciting one. To this day, positive feedback from families regarding my workshops is very fulfilling.

Parents and Children as Equal Stakeholders

I have identified some typical and more or less, ubiquitous issues with the current generation of parents and children.

Parents

Parents are a harried lot today. They are confused. They have very high aspirations for themselves and for their children.

1. **Paucity of time:** Many working mothers are hard-pressed for time. Striking work-life balance is a challenge. Fathers are pinned-down by long commuting and working hours.

   Although parents have all the right intentions, translating them into action, and I stress, 'right action' is a challenge. I always quote the example of how one nurtures a tree. First, telling yourself that you have to water it every day is not enough. The action has to happen. Second, you have to water the tree at the roots. Not a hundred yards away from it. Time and attention are crucial to nurturing children. Besides, parental attention and care is very essential during the early years of a child. The age up to twelve is the 'golden period'. This is when habits, attitudes and personality as a whole take shape. Bringing about a change in the child after this period is very, very difficult.

2. **Unrealistic Expectations:** Parents see children as an extension of themselves. They do not perceive them as individuals by their own right. Subconsciously, they posit all their aspirations on the children and expect them to play by their rules. Children are expected to be good at studies, sports, music and so on. They attend classes in the evening and on weekends too. How much can a child really take? They only end up being stressed; and their childhood is lost in the quagmire of expectations.

3. **Modern Parenting Practices:** Parents are confused about best practices. They are unsure of where to draw the lines. How much to indulge the child? When to discipline? How much to provide them?

Another issue is that parents are often at loggerheads about parenting styles and decisions. A consensus between the spouses is very essential. They must sit down and arrive at mutually agreeable decisions on how to raise their children. Otherwise, younger kids will be confused and older ones may take advantage of the situation.

Children

Children today are subject to too much exposure, too early. They barely understand or emote to all the stimuli that are bombarding them continuously.

1. **Technology** – The 21st century is the Age of Technology and Information. This has turned out also to be the biggest bane for the younger generations. Gadgets have disrupted the quintessential nature of childhood. Children's obsession with gadgets and unlimited access is alienating them from people and from reality. Screen time has replaced play-time. Online games and characters have replaced friends. Mental gymnastics has replaced physical activity. Somewhere along the line, our children are becoming less social, less humane, less emotional. A certain apathy and ennui is plaguing them. Living in the virtual world is wrenching our children off their emotions.

2. **The problem of excess** – Middle and upper-class children are born into luxury and comfort. So they don't know the value of money. Parents who have less time and more disposable income, are more than willing to swamp their children with 'things', be it toys, gadgets, edibles, clothes, accessories etc. They easily succumb to their demands. The child, at the end of the day is still dissatisfied, because materialism cannot bring

happiness and satisfaction.

3. **Sense of Entitlement** - Children today have imbibed a strong sense of entitlement. They feel that they deserve everything and that they should get it. They are not made aware that they need to put in their bit of effort and contribution to earn it. That is the reason you see children always compare, complain and are generally dissatisfied despite all the privileges.

4. **Freedom without responsibility** – Globalization, travel opportunities and media have given parents unlimited exposure to the world outside. Parents want their children to gain maximum exposure. They also want them to explore life experiences. In this excitement, parents are giving children unlimited freedom. However, they are failing to teach them the responsibility that comes with freedom; the responsibility to use freedom for constructive purposes; responsibility that is rooted in a value-based and ethical framework.

Approach – A Blend of Tradition and Science

If I have to look back and say, what is it about my approach that has ticked, then these are a few:

1. I adopt a scientific methodology. Having said that, I can also intuitively connect the dots to identify a pattern. A blend of these two is working well for me.

2. I feel parents must be aware of the developmental phases of a child. They will then know what specific emotional needs must be address at which stage.

3. Focus on the solution, not the problem – For instance, if a child is scoring low marks, the parent often attributes it to his lethargy, carelessness, distractions and inattentiveness. This is called focusing on the problem. Focusing on the solution would require the parent to analyze why the child is lethargic – is it food habits or is it excessive TV time, etc. and find solutions.

4. Identify the root cause of the problem, not just the manifestation or symptoms of the problem. For instance, why does a child display anger all the time? The symptoms would probably be shouting, using abusive language, throwing objects, breaking objects. You cannot solve the problem, if you focus on curbing or suppressing these behavior patterns. Hence, 'what' (the triggers) exactly is making the child angry should first be investigated and addressed.

5. Involve parents in the designing of the program, wherein, I try to leverage the strengths and weaknesses of both and help them complement each other to derive the best/maximum results from the program.

6. I stress on the power of communication in resolving issues. The channels of communication must be open between children and parents. The child must have the confidence and courage that she can express anything with her parents. Once the channels of communication are closed, alienation sets in. Parents will have no way to know what is running in the mind of their child or what the child is feeling.

Most parents struggle to maintain harmony in the family because there is no rulebook for parenting. Often all of us are trying the trial and error method and experimenting to find the right method.

Parenting Tips

Parenting can definitely be a joyous and enriching process if time and effort are invested.

Here are few pointers that parents can build upon in their approach to parenting.

- Establish a connection with your child. Connection comes through communication and emoting. With a free flow of conversation you and your child will be interested in each other's worlds and with interest comes empathy and understanding.
- Parents must be able to identify patterns exhibited by children and create awareness about the same in them.
- To understand the concept of disciplining children, and that discipline is not equivalent to punishment.
- Parents need to develop high levels of self-awareness in all aspects of life i.e. the physical, mental, social, emotional, spiritual and financial domains.

I find it fulfilling that my workshops can accelerate and facilitate individuals to live their dreams and fulfill their aspirations. Thus, as a Parent Coach and Educator, I deem it my responsibility to enable families to work as harmonious wholes so to build future societies that are healthy, strong and functional.

Sunitaa

Sunitaa is a Parent Coach from Bangalore, India. She has worked as an Educational Consultant for 8 years, helping children to bring best out of them. She understands child development and makes it easy for parents to understand it too. She also knows how hard it is to be a parent because she is a mother of two sons and has experienced challenges similar to those many families face today. Being a continuous learner helped Sunitaa to overcome her parenting challenges. With her knowledge and experience, she has helped many parents to restore harmony in their homes.

She is a 'Gold Medalist' in MSc - Plant Science and is working as a Parent coach from last 13 years. She strongly believes that parents have a powerful influence on their kids. Most parents think about their kids best interest at heart but often their actions might be misleading which leads to confusion and chaos. Sunita help parents to make their parenting journey enjoyable, serene and mindful. She provides a unique perspective to parents so that they are more aware and present in their parenting journey and develop a healthy parent-child relationship.

Sunita offers workshops and one-to- one coaching to support parents. She assesses individual needs and offers realistic suggestions based on each family's need. She helps them explore the reality of their family life, set realistic goals for the future and make an action plan of how to achieve these goals. She gives parents hands-on tools, strategies, and resources to build on children's innate strengths and potential while reducing the chaos, stress, and challenging behaviors.

Sunitaa approaches everyday with an attitude to make a difference. Her vision is to help parents in relishing their parenting journey, creating harmonious and productive families to nurture independent, confident and happy children.

7

HOW I GOT MY SUPERPOWERS AND CREATED MY IDEAL LIFE

How to re-think, re-design and re-launch your ideal life and business to produce significant influence and build an extremely profitable company

- BY JOHANN NOGUEIRA, FOUNDER AND CEO OF NOGUEIRA ALLIANCE PTY LTD

I was in trouble....

It was 2004. I was in the science laboratory, conducting experiments for my PhD. I'd spent the last five years of my life completing my Bachelor's degree to get to this point. I had achieved honours, been accepted into the most prestigious university in Melbourne (Australia), won a scholarship and proceeded to spend 16 hours a day in relative isolation, reading outdated literature, mapping out theories and looking forward to adding those two special characters before my name, that would tell the world I was a highly educated and successful man. My parents were going to be so proud of their son, Dr Nogueira.

Enter my supervisor. You see, he's one of Australia's top scientists. He has travelled the world speaking, writing papers, being interviewed, giving keynotes and is a highly respected authority in the industry. That is what I aspired to be. He had built his reputation and career on his hard work. He was in the office at 6am, went home at 6pm and was generally back at 8pm till midnight to continue his work. I told myself it would all be worth it. If I did this and followed suit, it would make me significant and respected. I would be someone.

Then everything changed and I remember that moment clearly. 11pm on a Friday night my supervisor walked into my lab and began to tell me what an amazing job I was doing and that my hard work would eventually pay off in 10 years. I considered his words and was happy to sacrifice 15 years of my life studying to achieve my doctorate and then work my way up the employment ladder. However, the conversation soon took an unexpected turn. Alas, I was about to break one of the rules my parents taught me.

"Never ask a man his wage or a woman her age".

I asked him "Would you mind telling me, how much money you make?" His reply completely took me by surprise as he stated an amount significantly less than I expected. I was shocked. In that moment my world came crashing down. If he was making that salary at his age and position, then all my dreams could never ever be achieved, even if I rose to his level. I was shattered, it was like being hit by a bus and I didn't sleep the next week…. (dramatic I know).

My subconscious mind was chaotic and searching for a way out, there had to be something else, there had to be another way to make the money I wanted.

Google: Make Money Online
Superpower acquired: Leverage and Systemisation

Those were the magic words I typed into Google that started me on a whole new journey. I had discovered eBay, found a product and saw that there was a margin, I put up my first auction and went to bed not knowing if anything worthwhile would come of this, but the next day I had made a profit of $20.

$20 DOLLARS! (while I slept) This is it…. Making money online actually works!!

I paused to consider the next step. If I was able to make $20, then what would it take to make $200 or $2,000 or even $20,000. I shifted my focus to repeating and scaling my initial success. In just a couple of weeks I had made $200 and within 6 months I was making more than my supervisor did in a year. Even better than that it took me only about 4-6 hours a week. It was incredible. I had found a way to create an income that would support my dreams.

My outlook changed completely as I realised that the answer was not about working harder, but working smarter.

During the day I continued my studies during the day and at night I'd spend my time learning new strategies to sell my products on the internet. I had managed to start an online business and learned to systemize and automate most of the processes. I felt very content but it only lasted for a month.

You see, I suffer from self-inflicted Attention Deficit Hyperactive Disorder (ADHD) and so I wasn't content with my newfound success. I wanted to do more with my spare time. I spoke to some of my online friends who were making money with affiliate marketing and decided it was time to try that. Looking back, I realise that time is the most valuable resource we have so spend it wisely.

Getting it RIGHT
Superpower acquired: Targeted marketing

Two years passed and my studies were now at the bottom of my priority list. My parents were furious and concerned that I spent all my time on my computer. I was excited as I had just hired a mentor to show me how to master affiliate marketing. Affiliate marketing is a process where you sell other people's products and get a commission for every sale generated, so essentially you are sending <u>the right people to the right offer at the right time.</u>

I was a learning machine, consuming information, running experiments online, split testing ads, imagery, copy, landing pages and different traffic sources. Every sale I generated sent me a needed dopamine kick directly into my brain, inflating my ego and my confidence.

I was addicted to results.

Soon Cost per Acquisition (CPA) marketing was mainstream and my competitive nature demanded that I master this too. This was <u>easier than affiliate marketing,</u> because you get paid for every lead you generate. No actual sale is required. So applying what I'd learned previously, I dived into CPA marketing and did very well, but it came at a cost.

The eagerness of something greater:
Superpower acquired: Balls to speak in front of strangers

It was 2008 and I sat in my apartment, unshaven in my pyjamas glued to my computer. I had evolved into a **recluse and an introvert.**

A phone call comes in. "Johann, I got your number from Mr 'X', I hear you are great at generating leads, I need your help". This businessman wanted me to generate leads for his seminar at the top of the Eureka tower. I took up the challenge and in two weeks I filled the room for Mr 'X' with 80 CEOs and Directors, he was so impressed that he offered me time the opportunity to speak at his event and when the moment arrived for me to stand up and talk, he introduced me with "Meet Johann, Because of this young man you are all sitting here".

This is the sort of introduction that many people would relish but the fact is, I was terrified of public speaking. The first time I did a presentation in front of just three people my hands were shaking, I was dripping in sweat and I nearly passed out. Now here I was, on stage at this man's event, clean shaven and suited up, with 160 eyes glued on me. From somewhere I found the courage to speak and told them about how the internet was going to change their businesses and their lead generation in the coming years and hence their lives.

They just stared back at me with blank looks and their mouths hanging open.

"I totally screwed up", so I thought.

But I didn't. I got a huge round of applause, lots of business cards with personal notes on them to "Call me" and some of the people hung around for two hours waiting to talk to me. Someone was feeling very significant that day.

The timing of destiny is perfect
Superpower acquired: Leading and designing my Dream Team

At this event, fate would have it that I met a man, who would contribute to my success and personal development. He had kindness in his eyes and wisdom in his speech, his experience and stories made me very humble. He was 60 years old and told me he came from a manufacturing background and had over 40 years of experience in business. With his experience and my skillset, we could do some great things he explained. The next day he rocked up to my house with a desk and his computer and said

"Let's Begin, and see what comes of it".

In a short period of time, just six months, we had built up the client base and we had teams offshore that were growing rapidly due to the workload. We were at capacity, overloaded and working 16 hour days to keep up with the work. So as a result we had to better systemize and automate our procedures and systems.

We started by building a website for each of our clients, turning it into an asset that would generating them leads. This led to more business for them, which in turn resulted in them want to spend more money on leads and automation. We did their branding, built their email campaigns, designed the clients' pathways through their business, setup their Ascending Transaction Models (ATM's), and their traffic sources for targeted marketing. Then designed or added software for their businesses to automate as much as possible and create touchpoints and top of mind awareness with their clients.

In short we designed, created, systemized and automated their entire business.

Our clients were getting results and were referring us to their friends. This was getting bigger than the two of us, so we decided that we needed support and a team of experts on the ground in Australia that shared our values.

We designed our dream team and started to interview people. We wanted the best and most experienced in their fields. We hired designers and graphic artists for the branding and web design, Conversion Rate Optimization (CRO) experts for the landing pages and split testing, Google search and display experts, Facebook marketing and engagement experts, copywriting experts and IT experts (as our online infrastructure grew and needed maintenance and support). We also hired specialist's in business development and mobile app creation, a support officer and a leading business strategist. We now had a formidable team of 80 staff offshore.

The Success trap
Superpower acquired: Letting go of the ego / Self evaluation and growth

We had clients, we had results, we had a great reputation. Things were going good and life was perfect. Or was it? The money was coming in and for all outward appearances we looked immensely successful, but we were spending it just as fast. I had a very poor understanding of financial planning and management and it felt like we would never get ahead. Later I married the love of my life who is a financial planner and boy did I get an education.

My ego was gone as I did not need to prove anything to anyone anymore. I found myself working from 6am till 6pm, having a quick dinner and then getting back to it and working until past midnight (remind you of someone?). My health was suffering, my time to learn and evolve had reduced to sweet diddly squat (nothing), my social life was non-existent and I was exhausted and feeling incomplete.

"How did I get here", I asked myself. "This is not my ideal life; I did not build this business to work IN the business...and be a slave to it. If I took a day off.... the business was an utter mess"

An evolution was required
Superpower acquired: Re-think; Re-design; Re-launch

So I sat down with my dear friends in search of advice. I also took time to listen to my virtual mentor Tony Robbin's and a couple of other inspiring individuals (talking to me through their programs, they always offered the right advice at the right time...thanks to the playlist button. Ultimately these particular people played a huge part in my life and I'd like to shake their hands and thank them, one day.

Things started to shift bit it was my wife who was the biggest catalyst for change. I decided to re-design my life, my relationships, and everything about me and my company. So we took a trip down the coast and spent two days in a beautiful hotel planning our lives. By the time we were done, we had filled books with how our relationship would be, what our friendship circles would look like, how our businesses would run, how we would raise our children, how our family life would be, where we would travel to, all our dreams and timelines to achieve them. It was an exhausting but productive and life changing weekend.

We implemented our plans, the company evolved and everything started to change. We were now dealing with clients on our terms, using our structured processes. Communication was the key and results were front of mind. The staff were happy, the clients were happy, the teams were happy and *I WAS HAPPY*. The company began to grow again. My health returned, my social life was reignited, my family was happy and we were getting big name clients.

Our reinvented, reinvigorated company was designed to achieve the following objectives:

- To help business owners establish, systemize and grow their businesses.
- To utilizing knowledge and learn from the masters in various industries so that we could learn and adapt strategies and tactics into our client's businesses.
- To give the business's founders the one thing they started their business for, freedom of choice to do what they wanted.
- To be the source of knowledge and experience that can help the clients prosper.
- To design their processes so that they have the right message delivered to the right people at the exact time they need it.

Not only has the company evolved, but my life has changed in extraordinary wasy and I have clarity around my WHY.

How did this help me achieve my goals?

My Why!
Not only has the company evolved, but my life has changed in extraordinary ways and I have clarity around my WHY.

- The business was systemized and now runs without me
- The foundations have been laid and this allows me to get involved with other companies that need the support of my skills and my company
- This allows me to travel and explore the world and meet interesting people

- It gives my family an amazing life....
- My son gets to grow up by my side (one of my major drivers, from early in life)
- I am fulfilled and complete

Is your WHY big enough
Superpower achieved: Speed to market

As soon as I knew what I wanted and WHY my dreams began to manifest. I have learnt that If an aligned goal is created, then a plan to achieve that goal can be put into place via habit and discipline formed from the 'Why'. The plan is then broken down into action steps and put across a timeline. This simple methodology allows you to take an idea and turn it into reality - simply follow the steps, one step at a time.

Fast forward to 2017, I now own multiple businesses. The systems we have built in one of the companies has had a major impact across communities and has revolutionised a whole industry (Buildings Management).

This new company, which is only one and a half years old, is setup to be listed on the stock exchange in a year's time, and this was only possible by surrounding myself with certain people who had specific skillsets (that I did not possess), who shared the grand vision and had the experience to take it to the next level. We all focus and build on each other's strengths and this allows us to reach and influence thousands of people and change their businesses and lives for the better.

Redesigning your life
Superpower achieved: Unsubscribe from the Matrix

Our lifespans are relatively short, but our minds and dreams are infinite and herein lies the problem. Most people's desires and dreams remain just that and never turn into reality. We all want to grow and experience new things but the timeframe we have to do it in, is very limited, especially if you are plugged into the matrix of normal society.

Think about when you leave your parents' nest and start to want things for yourself. It usually happens in your twenty's (for millennials the average age is now 35 years old), but most of the time, funds are limited, so you go to work or start a business. Then you spend the next 10 years establishing yourself in your chosen career or business. During your 30's for the majority of people, have kids and family life kicks in. Before you know it 40 is fast approaching.

Forty to fifty years old, is when entrepreneurs on average reap the rewards of their hard labour and employees are more relaxed about climbing the corporate ladder. In your fifties and sixties is where experiences are expected to be capitalized on, and soon after you are retired and reminisce of the time that has gone by so quickly. 70's -80's is where you enjoy the families that have been created due to your adventures in your youth and unfortunately soon after you head to meet your maker.

So my question for you …. is this the typical life you want to subscribe to or would you like to unsubscribe from the matrix and design your own?

The Future
Superpower in progress: Predicting/ Creating your future

My purpose while I'm on this Earth, is to influence and help as many people as possible to reach their full potential and live life on their terms. I have had the privilege to lead an amazing life (earned with multiple hard knocks, sweat and tears) and would like to share the rest of my journey with you.

Because of the people I meet and connect with, I'm fortunate to get access to information before it becomes mainstream. This helps in learning to forecast the future trends and take action to position myself, my companies and my clients in the right circumstances to thrive and leverage opportunities.

So if you have read this far, you have had a glimpse of my journey from my twenties through to my mid-thirties. I would love to connect with you and see if I can help you on your journey, or you with mine.

Over the next year, I'll be speaking, writing and video recording my teachings and experiences. If you would like to connect, head on over to http://JN.world and subscribe to my updates, download my app, like my facebook page, or watch my videos on YouTube - whatever social media you choose to devour content on.

> Let's continue this journey and let me help you re-think, re-design and re-launch
>
> your ideal life and business to produce significant influence
>
> and build an extremely profitable company.

To your unrelenting success,

Johann Nogueira

Johann Nogueira

As Founder and CEO of My Alliance Pty Ltd, Johann has spent his entire career solving problems and fixing businesses. He discovered of the power of systemization and leverage in his early 20's, where he built an ecommerce business, this knowledge allowed him to grow not only his business - but his clients as well. My Alliance now has a full time team of 80 people around the globe and 12 key people in Australia.

This has allowed Johann to invest and found other businesses that run systematically. One of his latest businesses has created a new standard in Apartment Building technology and will be present in smart buildings being constructed in Australia from 2017.

His technology and team give him an unfair advantage that allows solutions to be created to most problems presented.

Johann has significantly increased the bottom lines of over 1,000 clients in more than 40 industries, worldwide. He has dealt with most types of business and he thrives on studying, and solving, business questions, challenges and opportunities that are presented to him.

Johann's clients range from top tier banks to small business owners. But they all have one thing in common – all of them have profited significantly from his expertise.

He has identified the patterns that limit and restrict business growth. He is an industry leader who utilizes a myriad of marketing strategies from a variety of niches, instead of one particular marketing approach. He teaches that there may be dozens of more effective and more profitable strategies, and options, available to them.

Johann shows his clients how to take different success concepts from different industries and adopt them to their specific business. This gives his clients a powerful advantage over their competition. This skill set has captured the attention and respect of CEOs, best-selling authors, entrepreneurs and marketing experts.

Johann's four vital areas of implementation enhancement include Strategy, Innovation, Marketing, and Technology. He understands how to focus on the upside leverage within an organization, while effectively controlling and minimizing the downside risk. This has enabled him to find and successfully implement creative, pre-emptive, solutions to complex problems in order to generate high-performance results.

Johann's life's work has been dedicated to growing businesses, leveraging technology, and multiplying bottom lines. He believes strongly in ethical business practices and is a champion for anyone who wants to build their own business, advance their career, increase their personal wealth, and add to their personal growth.

You can connect with Johann via http://JN.World

8

MY PATH TO FREEDOM AND PURPOSE

- BY LISA SCOLNICK, LEAN MANUFACTURING SPECIALIST, CERTIFIED HIGH PERFORMANCE COACH, OPERATIONS LEADER

As a Lean Manufacturing Specialist, Industrial Engineer, and Certified High Performance CoachTM, I absolutely love my work. I enjoy the integration of process and people. When you truly engage the two, the results are significant. I'm known for my ability to double productivity and sustain it. Some credit goes to the methods; most goes to the people.

My first goal is to help my customers gain clarity around where to begin. Daily chaos and firefighting is common in manufacturing companies. After doing this work for 27 years, my eyes are trained to see patterns and problems. When I see these problems, I know the questions to ask to understand what caused it, what's happening around it, and what may happen downstream. After a plant tour, I boil it all down with the team, paint a picture of the current state, and develop strategies to achieve the future state. I can envision the perfect plant - machines operating, the people working, the material flowing through the plant. That's the technical side. On the people side, I assess the commitment from leadership and engagement of the people. Without those two things, real change is impossible. Sure, we can move forward anyway, but the problems will be painful to solve and the results will not be sustainable. It's very common to see Lean efforts crumble. It's because one of those two things either were never there or they stopped.

I've worked for many great companies through my career and learned different perspectives from each one. When I worked for Bristol-Myers Squibb, as a project manager implementing new products through operations, I learned about collaboration and culture. We were a truly high performing team of young adults that were empowered to make things happen. We didn't need to ask permission. We did what we thought was right. We didn't compete with each other because we all had the same goal. We were accountable to each other. The project management skills have served me in every position along the way.

After eight years and the announcement of our plant closing, I decided to work in the automotive industry. That's where I learned about Lean Manufacturing. Lean is a systematic approach to operational excellence, based on the Toyota Production System. I began just as the company began its Lean journey. I loved it and embraced it. Little did I know it would become the work I loved for many years. Implementations were happening across the entire plant of over 5,000 employees, from manufacturing cells and visual management to supermarkets and tugger routes. We were progressing very quickly. Looking back, I'm most grateful for seeing how all the applications and moving parts came together and worked as an integrated "system."

Although I worked for some great companies. I've always felt a deep desire for freedom. The freedom to decide how I was going to spend my time each day. I even longed to have just one day a week to get all my work done at home. I wanted to feel like I had everything under control. To leave no birthday card unsent, no laundry undone, or hockey game unattended. Unfortunately, I never worked for a company that offered part time work. It was all or nothing, and all meant 50+ hours a week. Working for manufacturing companies on shaky ground also left a dark cloud over my head, wondering whether or not I'd have a job the next day. Lay-offs were common and constantly lurking. I always knew I'd eventually become self-employed. I just didn't know when or how.

One day, as I was driving home from a major lay-off at work, I decided that I would never allow myself to be in that position ever again. I was going to create a life of choices. I dreamed of multiple revenue streams that I could tap into at any time. I wanted the ability to leave if I didn't like how I was treated. My husband had a good job, but we still needed two incomes. With two young children at home, I worried about paying the bills and saving for their education. I knew I'd work for myself one day. I also knew, in order to accomplish that, I needed an expertise that was in high demand. Fortunately, the company that had just laid me off gave me a tremendous amount of Lean Manufacturing experience, in addition to what I had in the automotive industry. I was leading a workshop every other week for almost two years. The job was high intensity and high stress. If you knew the woman in charge, you'd completely understand. As difficult as it was, I realized it was a gift. I learned so much, so quickly. It was the foundation I needed to begin my new journey.

As I look back, there were several philosophies and actions that had contributed to my success. I've identified ten areas that I am grateful for, either by learning them from amazing people or stumbling upon them during challenging times. It is my honor to share my experience and perspective with you.

1. **Mastery of my topic. Life-long learning.** I believe a key component to my success is my never-ending drive toward mastering Lean Manufacturing. Over time, I grew more and more passionate and eager to teach others. Lean can be complex. There are so many tools to learn and ways to connect them together. Each application is so different, requiring a lot of thought to understand the problem, how to approach it, in what order, as well as how to engage the people. Over the last 19 years, I've remained a good student, even today. There are always more methods to learn, approaches to take, ideas to see in action. I still get excited about learning something new from a book, video, or seminar on Lean. What topic are you passionate about?

2. **What is the next tool I need to learn?** Go get it. I paid very close attention to where I struggled. I asked myself what skills or knowledge I needed. How could I develop the skill? I was willing to do whatever it took to learn the material. I attended a few training courses. Since I knew the training budget would be limited, reading books became the best solution for me. I was very intentional about my book selection. I read what I needed at the time. I applied immediately to test what I had learned. I've read well over 140 books, some of them multiple times. I even took a speed-reading course to take in the information quicker. Today, I still love to learn through books.

3. **Grasp the situation.** Step one to becoming a good problem-solver. One of the lessons I learned very early on was the concept of "Grasp the Situation." When we're assigned a project, we sometimes feel the urgency to jump right in. That's actually one of the worst steps we can take if we're not familiar

with the problem or scenario. I believe I found this path out of fear and desperation. I learned this when I worked in the fast-paced, challenging automotive industry. Production was serious business. The demands on time and outcome were high. The consequences of not performing were, let's just say, not pretty. The only way I could get my arms around understanding my job was to spend time on the shop floor and ask the Operators a lot of questions. I felt I needed to understand how the HVAC unit was built, so I began at the head of the line, met every Operator, and asked them to explain their part of the assembly. By the time I reached the end of the line, which took almost two weeks, I knew how to build an HVAC unit AND I knew every single Operator by name. They also got to know me. By grasping the build process and connecting with the Operators, I created a perfect scenario to do a great job. The two week investment up front allowed the rest of my work to flow smoothly. That lesson I carried over to every job that followed.

4. **Connecting to people.** My true love is connecting with people on the shop. I know how to engage them. When I see Operators, Tradesmen, and Technicians, I see my Dad. He was a Tradesman for 41 years. He's my hero. He taught me that the people are key to success. Being vulnerable and asking for help is one of the ways. This helps them see that I'm sincere and authentic. We create a team of mutual respect. No competition, just high levels of collaboration where everyone feels valued for their contributions. I teach them the tools, they teach me reality on the floor. We create it together. When people are involved in the creation of their processes, they follow it. When it's pushed on them, they don't. It's that simple. I remember one very kind Operator who made a confession to me after we completed our project. He said, "I wasn't sure whether this would work or not. But you were really nice, so I thought I'd at least give you a chance. Now I

see it. It really does work well."

5. **Find work that is more challenging or unique.** I only take on work that I'm qualified to do, but I like to make sure it requires me to stretch. Whether it's an application I've never experienced or there's a big challenge present, those are my favorite assignments. I like there to be an element of discomfort in it. I also go in with the mindset that failure is not an option. My clients are counting on me to lead the way. This forces my to step up. Collaborate with other people. Figure it out, often within a short timeframe. I like to refer to these projects as "juicy."

6. **Having confidence in my skills and myself.** I know that every problem has a solution. It's just a matter of figuring it out. That's a powerful mindset. Each stretch experience contributed to the solid foundation. Over time, I gained the confidence to walk into any plant, any office, and any project. What I didn't know, I knew the people would know. All I had to do was be kind and respectful and ask the right questions. We'd figure it out together. Each assignment gave me experience and perspective that I could use in the future. It was like carrying around a toolbox. Sometimes I'd pull out a single tool. Most of the time, I'd pull out several tools, mix them together, add something new, and create an entirely new tool to put back in my toolbox. Know and trust in your ability to figure it out.

7. **Self-employment.** Becoming self-employed was one of the scariest decisions I had ever made. But, it really wasn't much different than the threat of losing my job. The difference was that I was able to plan, prepare, and leave on my own terms. I began by taking small projects and using some vacation time. I also did work on evenings and weekends. This helped me build a financial cushion before the big leap. With my plans in place,

all I needed was one decent-sized contract. Then one day, in 2008, it happened – a signed contract. My husband almost had a heart attack, but he was very supportive. I'll never forget his response, "Wow. You're really doing this, aren't you? I know I can't stop you. Ok. You work really hard. I know you'll figure it out and make it work." I love that man!

8. **Expertise in a Big Way.** I loved the freedom of self-employment, but I was still trading time for money as a consultant. I needed to find a better way. My new path began when I found Brendon Burchard, founder of Experts Academy. At my first event, I learned two things: 1) the expert space 2) the value of including a scalable component to my business. That's when I decided to create on-line training programs to get my expertise out there in a big way to help even more companies. I was always positive and determined to make it work. I attended seminars, learned a great deal, and met amazing people. The challenge was time. I still worked full time during the day. My evenings and weekends were filled with kids' sports and domestic duties. Where was I going to find the time to make all this happen? I wasn't getting very much sleep, my eating habits were inconsistent. I ate healthy food, but I also ate a lot of junk, primarily sugar. Overall, I was stressed without clarity on exactly where I was going. That's when I realized I needed to work on myself and improve my personal performance.

9. **Get a Coach.** I seriously wish this was the first step I took. The journey would have been so much easier, because I would have been physically and mentally prepared for it. I had great intentions, but I got stuck. I didn't have a solution or the skills to break the cycle myself. The game changer for me was High Performance CoachingTM. Since I was already a student of Brendon Burchard, I knew this was the answer. I attended the inaugural class of Certified High Performance CoachingTM.

Through the course, I not only became a coach, I also received coaching. I realized the only thing standing in my way was me. I didn't have crystal clear Clarity about where I was going. I wasn't managing my energy levels, which led to many unproductive hours. I didn't have the courage to take a few critical steps that were the key to moving forward. Even as a productivity expert, I didn't know how to truly tap into my personal productivity until I learned the habits and tools. High Performance CoachingTM was the key that opened the door to my next level of success. Coaching helped me perfect my habits so that I could perform at my highest levels. When I experience bumps in the road, I have greater control over my thoughts to work through solutions with more ease. Today, High Performance CoachingTM allows me to help people achieve breakthrough levels of performance.

10. **Find Your Tribe.** Traveling on a new path is scary. I often felt alone and isolated, especially since no one else in my personal life could relate to my challenges. That's why finding my tribe was critical. It wasn't intentional on my part, but once we met through a mastermind group, we realized the deep connection and value of having each other. We are like-minded people pursuing similar goals and dreams. We understand the challenges and help each other avoid or work through them. We fully celebrate each other's successes because we truly know what it took to get there. We are family.

Through the work that I do and the people I reach each day, I have a strong sense of purpose. I want to be remembered as someone who saw greatness in people who didn't see it in themselves. As someone who helped people develop their gifts, take courageous steps, and use their talents for their true purpose and meaning in life. I'm passionate about making sure people are treated well, especially in the workplace, to make sure their abilities aren't buried and wasted. I believe when people are ignored, excluded, or judged, they lose sight of their value. They forget who they really are. I think it's common. It's very sad. Everyone has the ability to see others' strengths, especially when we intentionally look for them.

Thank you for the opportunity to share my story with you. I hope I've helped and inspired you on your journey. If I can help you in any way, please visit my website www.LisaScolnick.com, download tools, and feel free to reach out to me. If you've enjoyed my story or have questions, I'd love to hear from you. I wish you the best on your path to success and happiness.

Lisa Scolnick

Lean Manufacturing Specialist, Certified High Performance Coach™, Operations Leadership

Process improvement without the people leads to failed attempts at business transformation. Motivating people without the science behind it leads to immeasurable results that disappear when the excitement fades. Combining the two adds jet fuel to your company's performance.

Yes, the methodologies are powerful, but without commitment from leadership and buy-in from the people, the results are never sustainable. I believe the magic lies in connecting the hearts and minds of each and every employee.

"My Dad was a tradesman for 41 years. When I told him I decided to become an Industrial Engineer, this was his response…"Whatever you do, take care of those people. Listen to them. They know more about the product and machines than anyone else in the company." At the time, I had no idea he had handed me the key to my success."

As a facilitator and coach, Lisa Scolnick has spent 27 years helping companies redesign processes to achieve Operational Excellence and increased productivity. She is the founder of LisaScolnick.com. Her primary methods include Lean Manufacturing and High Performance CoachingTM.

Having worked in a broad range of industries and offices, Lisa has the expertise and confidence to achieve results in even the most complex and unique applications. She is known for her ability to double productivity. In manufacturing plants, she creates solid systems and high levels of productivity. In offices, she takes the mystery out of transactional work and defines the operational levers needed to create stability. Lisa pulls it all together with High Performance CoachingTM, which helps individuals and teams master the personal skills known to the world's most successful people: Clarity, Energy, Courage, Productivity, and Influence.

Lisa works at both strategic and tactical levels, quickly seeing the opportunities, connecting the dots, and painting a picture that all levels of the organization can embrace. It's easy to connect with her contagious passion and warmth. Leaders love her vision, strategies, execution, and results. The people love her friendly, engaging, and respectful interactions.

Lisa is a native of Buffalo, New York and continues to live there with her family. In addition to her Operations work, she is very passionate about personal development. She loves to help people become the best version of themselves, as well as find their true purpose and meaning in life. Her warm, friendly, and caring personality makes her easy to trust. She takes a compassionate, yet challenging approach to High Performance CoachingTM. After coaching dozens of individuals, she's proud to share that each of her clients has experienced significant breakthroughs and life changing transformations.

Throughout her career, she has won several awards for her

achievements including (2) Bristol-Myers Squibb President's Awards and a Visionary of the Year Award from Wilson Greatbatch.

Lisa earned her Master of Business Administration (1997) and Bachelor of Science in Industrial Engineering (1990) degrees from the State University of New York at Buffalo. Lisa is also a Certified High Performance Coach™, Certified Six Sigma Black Belt, and a Certified Workplace Big Five Personality Profile™ consultant.

Lisa is married to her husband, Mike, of 24 years. She's also the proud mom of Derek (21) and Sarah (19). After recently ending two decades of kids' sports, Lisa's now ready to change the world. And, yes, she really does miss the hockey bag smell in her trunk.

9

WHY I FAILED 541 TIMES?

Failure is simply the opportunity to begin again, this time more intelligently.
Henry Ford

- BY VISHWANATH KOKKONDA, PH D -
ENTREPRENEUR, ENTERPRISE TRANSFORMATION (SAFE) & BUSINESS ACCELERATION CONSULTANT AND COACH

On hindsight, I understand that for me entrepreneurial success has been a result of intense introspection and continuous learning. My entrepreneurial dreams came to fruition through a company, Yagnaum systems that I co-founded along with my brother Gopinath Kokkonda. We are a solutions integrator and consulting firm specializing in technology and staffing solutions for organizations in the publishing, new media, finance, lifestyle, retail and education sectors. To reach this level of success, which essentially to me means, fulfilling my own aspirations in life, was a roller coaster ride, with unexpected turns and twists, at times racing and at others stagnating. The company name Yagnaum is made of two Sanskrit words, Yagna symbolizing sustained effort with intense focus to achieve a positive cause and Aum representing divine energy united in its three elementary aspects: creation, preservation and liberation.

***

Know Thyself

When you know yourself, you are empowered!

False confidence and assumptions about one's self and one's capabilities often mar the growth and evolution of an individual. A realistic feedback from the people you interact with goes a long way in creating a realistic perception of yourself. This has been the greatest discovery of my life.

To substantiate what I mean, I have to take you back in time. I hail from Warangal, a tier-2 city, 120km from Hyderabad. I was a bright and intelligent child. People around me assumed that I would do very well in all aspects of life; score well in every exam; get admission for a course of my choice; in short, become anything I aspired to be. I let this

---

How do you validate your assumptions?

What is the process for creating a valid assessment of your current capabilities and future potential?

CLARITY IS THE MANTRA!

- **Thought:** Observe and identify recurrent though patterns. Understand the basis of these thoughts; categorize them based on priorities and skills; eliminate unproductive and destructive thoughts.
- **Belief:** Identify and understand the basis of your beliefs; categorize them as: strong, not sure, weak. Strengthen beliefs, which have helped you evolve and accept them validate them.
- **Attitude:** Attitude is the culmination of thoughts and beliefs. A thought, when converted into a belief remains entrenched in the mind. Your attitude determines your perception and assessment of external stimuli. Analyze and revise underlying thoughts and believes to change attitude.
- **Personality** – A complex combination of all the attitudes of an individual makes his personality. To bring about a change in the personality, change has to begin at the level of belief and attitude.
- **Behavior** – Behavior is the person's response to external stimuli in accordance with attitude. So behaviour is the external manifestation of the personality.

Thus clarity helps align your thoughts, beliefs and actions with your aspirations, based on assumptions, validation and corrective action.

assumption percolate into my mind, unquestioned. I began to assume that I could, in fact, achieve all that I ever wanted. However, I did not know then that I also had to work, work very hard towards achieving a goal. With every attempt, I failed. When I say I failed, I do not mean that I failed an exam or that I was out of work at any point in time. In fact, I have never failed an exam. What I do mean is that I failed to achieve any goal or dream. In fact, the goal or dream did not even emerge out of conviction and passion. I set goals randomly, based on what the ecosystem of people around me said.

People assumed I would become a doctor since my father was a doctor. I assumed so too, without even asking myself if that is what I wanted. I wanted it because everybody around me wanted it. I missed medical college admission by a whisker. Some basic doubts in physics and chemistry haunted me all through my 10+2 education, I never sought anybody's help to get them addressed, as my assumption that If I ask basic doubts I would lose my image of intelligent boy. I feel so silly about that attitude, then. I joined B.Sc. Life sciences for no rhyme or reason. I did not even attend college. I aimed for Indian Administrative Services (IAS). Then I pursued MBA and instead of joining up work like all my friends, I prepared for civil services exam. I failed to clear the final level. Didn't have patience to pursue further with assumed justifications such as all civil servant jobs are bribe filled with little independence. I never clarified. This non clarifying behavior pattern dominated by self-thinking and decision making pattern prevailed.

I should say, I am little too much social with interests in many things including politics, psychology, music, films, philosophy, sports and business. I engage myself in the above stated in the form of reading, thinking and discussing with people in my network. It happens till date that I instantly appeal to people around me with my versions and interpretations. Not everytime and always, though. People continued to praise me. It got into my head. I was delusional. I thought I was born for bigger things. That is the quintessential aspirational quality in me. However, I did not realize that I had neither the requisite skills nor the diligence to achieve anything big

Then, I went to U.K to pursue MS in information technology. Failure beat me black and blue. Pursued career in SAP Consulting. Worked for couple of World's best companies including one of big four. My rich learnings ever from those working stints with global conglomerates and few of fortune 500 clients are invaluable. But the string feeling that I am made for something big continued to prevail putting me to inconvenience with the procedural progress. I thought (assumed) I am ripe enough to make my mark through entrepreneurship. I jumped into entrepreneurship; once again aiming for the stars, with neither the capability nor the understanding. I made no profits; just managed to sustain the business. I gave it some time, but things did not look up.

> **How do you validate your assumptions about yourself?**
>
> You are your best judge. Find your inner mentor. Validation is a self-centric process. Constantly test yourself at short intervals about how close you are to your goals. Your performance and results must match the level of achievement you are aspiring for. If you can do that consistently, you can validate whether your assumptions are correct.

Transition – A Spiritual Awakening

I abruptly decided to take a break; do nothing at all. This was a period of intense anxiety and introspection. For the first time I realized that something was wrong in my approach to life itself. I had to figure out why I failed so consistently. Where was I going wrong?

Introspection led me on the path of truth:

a) I was operating on assumptions about myself that were validated neither by me, nor by the ecosystem around me.

b) Success will not land at my feet. I have to work hard to achieve success.

There was a deep chasm between what I was and what I thought I could be. Learning to bridge this gap was my only salvation. I realigned my thoughts and actions.

A spiritual experience is not some profound out of body experience. It is just a new perspective to your inner self. Isn't that the greatest experience for mankind? Isn't that the most difficult task to achieve?

My Pursuit for Perfection

All along, even as I was doing things randomly I was also doing other things out of my own volition, for which neither I, nor the ecosystem gave any importance. For instance, I read voraciously. My home was a mini library. My father Dr Premnath, a retired medical doctor had a large collection of books. He initiated the reading habit when I was around 12 years old. I read nearly 3,000 books till now, mostly pertaining to philosophy and psychology in a short span. My stint with India's initiative National Cadet Corps (NCC) is one of the most cherishable one - I was chosen as Andhra-Pradesh State's 'Best Candidate' in the air-wing division and I was invited to participate in the RDC parade in New

> During this phase, I mastered various skills:
>
> - Knowledge – Discipline -Hard work
> - How to arrive at vision, mission and objectives
> - How global organizational leaders drive organizations
> - Project pipeline building strategies
> - How to compete for projects with specific USPs
> - Professional project handling
> - Compliance meeting measures
> - To add value to clients
> - People management and competitive HR practices
> - World's best practices in each of the above
>
> A realigned perception of myself and skill development laid a strong foundation for my

Delhi. On hindsight, I understand that all the random things I did, have made me what I am. Failures made me pursue excellence.

I changed six jobs, each requiring different skill sets. I did not enjoy any one of them. In the meantime, I pursued Ph.D and Masters in Psychology. I earned certifications in Scaled Agile (SAFe), Scrum, Business Excellence Assessor (CII), Six Sigma Black Belt (KPMG), Business Analytics (ISB – EE), SAP Logistics (SAP AG), Astrology and Hindustani Music. There was absolutely no pattern to what I was doing.

During my stint in professional Jobs at Reliance Industries, Deloitte Consulting India, and IBM, I learned a lot. Those were world- class organizations and I am very fortunate to have been part of them.

The taste of Success

Success, when it finally came in the form of Yagnum Software, was all the more sweet. I have now transcended the entrepreneurial role to business performance accelerator, coach, speaker and investor.

Mentor and Coach

All along, I have been very good at communication and networking. I have maintained good working relationships with people, which has created a good pipeline for conducting workshops on Agile, six sigma, business analytics, digital marketing, and business excellence among others. I conduct about 6-7 sessions every month. I have also performed career-counseling shows on television.

Social Service

I dedicate most of my weekends for social service. I have been part of Lions Club International since 2012 and have impacted more than 7000 lives directly and indirectly through health camps. I am associated with a social service organization based in Hyderabad, where I am a senior office bearer. Lions Club is celebrating its Centenary next year and aims to empower 25 million youth as part of its centenary project. I have empowered over 10,000 students in the areas of employability and entrepreneurship. I have been conducting employment sessions, up-skilling etc., for 18-22-year-old students in and around Hyderabad.

I was chosen as Melvin Jones Fellow by Lions Club International for exceptional service to humanity and Outstanding Zone Chairperson Of 2015 – 16 of Lions District 320 A.

I am a visiting faculty for over 30 odd Engineering and Business colleges in Andhra-Pradesh. I am on the academic boards of Woxsen Business School, Hyderabad and Vaagdevi College of Business Management, Warangal.

I am the Honorary Business Advisor at ACPM Consulting, Unistring Solutions, NSS Communications and ONS IT Solutions.
I am a training consultant to National Small Industries Corporation (NSIC) and an active member of their training consultants' panel.

I have over 6 publications in Indian journals, 2 international conference papers and my thesis is mid-way to be published as a book.

Learning and Advice to youngsters

Planning, Preparation and Action-oriented approach are the only path to success. For example, to sit in one place and think with a positive approach 'I will get this job', 'I will clear this exam' will not ensure that you get the job or clear the exam. You have to plan, prepare and actually study to clear the exam. Likewise, you have to assess your skills and knowledge level for the job. If you find yourself falling short of the job requirements, ensure you gain those skill sets and the technical knowledge required. Therefore, to think positively is not enough, but you must act positively. Having said that, positive thought is the basis for positive action.

Success would not have been valuable if I had not failed. Do not get bogged down by the pace of the journey of your peers. Each person's pace is different.

Compete with self and no one else. Overtake yourself consistently. Look around. See the benchmarks. Get inspired. Park it in your mind. Leave it there.

Your progress depends upon right assumptions about yourself.

The Phoenix

The metaphor of the Phoenix bird, from Greek mythology, is my guide. The Phoenix rises from its own ashes. It is a perfect metaphor for my belief: failure is positive; to rise from failure is positive thinking. And the only path to rejuvenation!

Vishwanath Kokkonda, Ph D - Entrepreneur, Enterprise Transformation (SAFe) & Business Acceleration Consultant And Coach

Vishwanath alias Vish, at present is leading co-founded IT solutions integration and staffing firm from based in US, UK and India from Hyderabad. His 22+ years of experience comprises of working stints with few World's top notch firms including one of big 4, few fortune 500 firms and a tech start-up. He catered to manufacturing, retail, food & beverages, oil & gas and automobile Industry sectors in domains which include market research, utility sales, SAP Logistics consulting, Mobile apps, recruitment and staffing, analytics, digital marketing, business excellence consulting and quality consulting.

He is complemented by Certifications in SAP Logistics, SAFe SPC 4 (Scaled Agile), Six Sigma, Business Analytics, Scrum, EFQM Business Excellence - Ph D in Business Management, MBA, M Sc (Psychology), Diploma in IT & Astrology. His publications include 6 national and 2 international conference papers.

Vish is empanelled by few Telugu television channels on their talk shows related to personal productivity and he is acting guest faculty to some prominent professional colleges in and around Hyderabad. For social work through World's largest NGO comprising of 1.4 million lion members, Vishwanath was awarded Melvin Jones Fellowship (MJF) for his conviction towards human service in the form of health camps, food distribution and empowerment programs in rural and slums areas in and around Hyderabad. Empowered 9000 odd people in last 5 years in the areas of employability skills, entrepreneurship skills and productivity enhancement skills. To study, work and for holiday, vishwanath visited UK, Germany, France, Switzerland, Japan, China, Singapore, South Africa, Thailand, Indonesia, SriLanka and Nepal.

10

THE WORLD IS AT YOUR FOOTSTEPS

"The world is the true classroom. The most important and rewarding type of learning is through experience; seeing something with our own eyes."

- BY AMIT PUNJABI, BUSINESS COACH, MENTOR AND FOUNDER OF SANKALP ACADEMY

It's strange but at a very young age, I discovered that there is a lot to learn in the world than in the confines of a classroom. This was not the mindless ramble of a teenager bored at school, but of a boy who had experienced and absorbed learning in all its wholesomeness outside institutional learning. At the age of 16, I had started doing odd jobs for pocket money. One such was to help organize an event. I worked for an event manager. It was a conference, and I got the opportunity to listen to some fantastic speakers. I felt I had learned a lot in those two hours than in the several hours I had spent inside the classroom. I decided then that I had to 'step out' into the world and out of my comfort zone if I had to learn in the true sense of the word. This was a transformational moment that shaped my attitude and personality.

Another event that enhanced my self-confidence was, ironically, when I failed in 12th grade. All along I was busy helping in organizing seminars, workshops etc. When I failed, my relatives shamed me and suggested I join the family business, as is the case with boys who failed in studies. My parents stood by me and said, although he has failed in his exams, he is very well equipped to handle the vagaries of life. He will still be very successful. They said that unlike other kids of my age, I did not spend free time with friends or playing or did not demand a bike or other expensive things. But I was working hard, earning and learning all that I could in my part time jobs.

My own life experiences are the inspiration behind the philosophy of Sankalp Academy. At Sankalp Academy, we are driven by the desire to help people discover and achieve their potential. Two traits that have contributed to the person that I am today are: my readiness to break through inhibitions and my ability to handle freedom with responsibility.

Break Free

In my interactions with people, I have realized that a vast majority of them are stuck in their comfort zone. They do not want to step out of their shell. Reasons can be many, lack of awareness, lack of confidence, self-imposed inhibitions, fear of failure and so on. But only if you take the first step towards change, will you know what you are capable of, isn't it? If you remain in your shell, you have to satisfy yourself with a mediocre life.

Freedom and Responsibility

Young adults crave for freedom. But can they handle it? With freedom comes responsibility. Otherwise, freedom can become a burden. My parents gave me freedom at a very young age. I nurtured that freedom with great responsibility.

Programs at Sankalp

One of the most successful and widely acknowledged workshops 'Adventure Leadership Camp' is designed to assist people to break through their mindset of fear and limitations. Changing the mindset of a person is the most difficult to achieve. But once they initiate the change within, they can achieve unprecedented success in their personal and professional lives. I would like to quote the example of a lady, a victim of sexual abuse, who had feared darkness for 14 years of her life. She was able to break through this fear in less than half a day.

Innovative Leadership is a program that helps one to generate ideas. According to the most successful people on the planet, you cannot sit and wait for opportunities to come your way, but you have to create them. Results, Outcomes and Success can only be generated from tools, events and opportunities that you have created. Your ability to succeed will always depend on your ability to innovate. The Innovative Leadership Workshop is a platform where every individual develops the ability to create value and success generating resources.

I cannot emphasize enough the importance of effective communication skills. So we have a Communication program, the focus of which is to help people connect with other people, not just listen or speak or write. We offer a program on Neuro Linguistic Programming (NLP). NLP is a philosophy and an educational tool, which is designed to teach people how to become happier and more effective. It teaches people how to think and communicate in more useful ways. It explores HOW we think and HOW we behave. It allows you to discover what is going on when you are doing something well and not doing something well. It allows you to find out how other people do things effectively. NLP is fast becoming one of the most sought after tools of human enhancement and performance improvement that has ever been known. Science Digest describes NLP as 'the most important synthesis of information available today about human communication'.

We have a program called Build The Home Team, which is targeted at families.

The aim of all these programs is 'realization'; a change in perspective. For instance, a 61-year-old scientist attended our program, after being frustrated with his career for 28 years of his life. Through our program, he realized he wanted to get into training because he enjoyed interacting with and training people. But he did not know how to get into the industry. With our inputs, he decided to do what he enjoyed and so joined a leading MNC as the head of training.

We had another 11-year-old girl from Chandigarh. At that tender age, she was addicted to Hindi television serials and had very low confidence because she could not speak fluent English. After undergoing our program, she not only moved from television serials to reading books but also gained enough confidence to become the Vice Captain of her School.

Trends in the Industry

The training industry if I may call it so is undergoing a positive transformation. The four trends I can identify as an insider are:

Learning needs have now become a lifestyle. It's more about enhancing your personality and not just about readiness for a particular job.

The focus is on engaging people rather than just reaching out: Industry Experts have reached out to a lot of people through workshops, seminars and conferences for several decades now. However, not a lot of people have been able to take back strategies and learning to apply to real life challenges. Reaching out has helped people gain information, but has not facilitated in the development of Attitude and Leadership. The trend now is to actually engage with people and get them involved in a certain system to take action. It isn't just about talks, seminars and conferences, but it is also about smaller workshops and discussion groups where people get coached on engaging in action-oriented behavior and achieving identifiable results.

Training areas are becoming more focused rather than being generic. From generic Communication Skills, we have moved over to probing skills, skills of persuasion, presentation skills, cross-cultural communication and so on.

The world today is very dynamic. The pace of change in every walk of life and business is so fast, that one has to keep updating oneself from time to time. In that sense, there is a lot of scope in the industry. We as trainers have to be ahead of the times, updating ourselves of what is happening in the world, identifying training needs, developing training material accordingly. For instance, statistics show that 300 new professions are coming into existence every year, requiring diverse skill-sets! The Top 10 skillset requirements of 2015 didn't even exist in 2005, such as App Developer, Cloud Computing Services and Social Media Manager to name a few!
(http://www.forbes.com/sites/meghancasserly/2012/05/11/10-jobs-that-didnt-exist-10-years-ago/2/#396905f49b5b)

I think these are brilliant for the growth of the industry and can definitely add more value to the participant. So, that again brings me back to my core belief that there are plenty of opportunities in the world outside. But you have to step out of the shell that you have created around yourself to be able to see and explore them. The shell is only an illusion. It exists only in the mind. So the transformation has to occur within. WE are only facilitators.

Challenges

Like any other industry, this industry is also fraught with many challenges. The foremost being it is filled with self-proclaimed trainers who claim superiority over others. They fail to understand, that in this industry there is no scope for competition. We may all be training on the same topics, but our methodologies and outcomes are different. Ultimately, the takeaway and value-add for the participant are what matters and what ensures your survival. But it is difficult to judge until you have completed the training itself.

Another challenge is participants expect transformation or learning by passive attendance at the workshop or training session. They often do not realize that until and unless they are proactively involved, and internalize what is being said by the trainer, they cannot achieve transformation. The effectiveness of a program is proportional to the receptiveness of the participant. The fact that a particular participant has taken the initiative to enroll is the first step towards realization. Because most of the times, one is not even aware of one's shortcomings. So if that barrier is broken, half the job is done. Having said that, the rest is also very crucial.

A lot of people confuse public speaking with coaching. Not all public speakers can coach individuals on skills required to lead a successful life. A lot of times, great public speakers fail to add value in one-to-one conversations and basic coaching methods.

Another challenge that exists is the availability of self-help books. It is one thing to read them and completely another to use what is in the book to transform yourself or coach other individuals. There are a lot of people who are trying to become coaches by reading experiences of others in books. However, a person becomes an effective coach by generating value from his/her own experiences rather than just others' experience.

Social media, although, has changed the way we communicate, is a limiting factor for our industry, because, it kills curiosity and experiential learning. It is inundating us with mere 'information'. Even your school text books give you information. But mere information does not translate into learning for the practical world. Besides, the information that you read is not even factually correct most of the times. I'll give an example of how social media can be misleading. I am a huge fan of Bhagat Singh. I read up a lot about him. A buzz started on social media that February 14th, which happens to be Valentine's Day, was also the day Bhagat Singh was hung. In fact, he was hung on the 23rd of March. People blindly believed. So that's the threat from social media. If people are not curious, they stop growing.

Entrepreneurial Success

AS an entrepreneur you have to learn to prioritize what is important for you in your journey. You may not have the time to accommodate many things in your life. For instance, in my teen years and thereafter, I sacrificed all my weekends. I never met friends nor partied with them. Never relaxed. Any free time, I was out working, learning new things, interacting with people who were successful professionally and personally. Sundays were exclusively reserved for meeting successful people. I networked during events or simply over LinkedIn and requested for appointments. I just spoke, discussed and interacted with them.

This willingness to grow is the next important trait for an entrepreneur. You must set targets – personal and professional – and do all that is necessary to achieve them. Stagnation will surely throw you out of business. Weekdays I did what I 'had to do' and weekends I did what I 'wanted to do'.

To beat stagnation and competition, you have to be open-minded --- to learn and innovate. As I said earlier, if you have to survive, you have to constantly innovate and that requires a curious mind, keenness, and creativity. Devise better programs, better methods and techniques of executing them.

Triggering 'realization' and the 'transformation' it engenders is what motivates me. I am very happy that my profession is also my passion, whereby I can make a difference to peoples' lives, in whatever small way possible.

Amit Punjabi, Business/Life coach and Founder of Sankalp Academy, established it in 2008. It is a Training & Coaching organization committed to empower people to live a life driven by choice than circumstances. Since 2008, he has been conducting training programs on NLP Skills, Communication, Leadership, Life Strategizing & have trained and coached people from different walks of life in producing extra-ordinary results both in their personal & professional life. A certified NLP trainer, Master Practitioner & Life Coach / Strategist, Amit has worked with individuals, students & professionals to help them produce extra-ordinary results in their lives since 2006.

Amit is a young, inspiring and passionate trainer/coach whose passion lies in building and moulding ordinary individuals into extraordinary leaders. At the young age of 20, He stepped out of the traditional family mould and kick started Sankalp Academy – A training and coaching organization with an investment of ₹ 700 and one full tank of fuel in his bike. Since then there has been no looking back. He has personally lead and mentored organizations, and youth movements impacting over 45,000 people (Students & Professionals) in a short span of 9 years.

His passion to help people design lives could only be matched with his desire to consume knowledge. An avid learner he is a certified NLP Trainer & Master Practitioner and a certified Learning Skills Coach.

As a Business Coach, he has mentored and helped numerous start ups gain tremendous and stable results through designing strategies that they can apply to their individual businesses.

Facebook - www.facebook.com/thesankalpacademy
Twitter - twitter.com/sankalpacademy
Instagram - www.instagram.com/thesankalpacademy/

11

THE PATH TO STOCK MARKET SUCCESS
- BY ADRIAN REID, STOCK TRADING COACH, STOCK TRADING EDUCATOR

An early dream lost... then found

Freedom is what I've always dreamed about. The financial freedom to explore, play and learn and pursue things that fascinate and interest me.

I strongly suspect that this dream started when I was 9 years old and spent many hours playing an old board game called "The Stockmarket Game".

I remember playing and amassing great fortunes as soon as I figured out a profitable strategy for the game. It was a race between my siblings and I to accumulate millions of dollars and huge stock portfolios and dividend streams from these portfolios...so from a very early age I was hooked on the stock market.

But somewhere along the way I lost that dream.

Seduced by the professional world and the apparent prestige of the corporate ladder I found myself working countless hours a day on someone else's dream. Striving to make the partners from the consulting firm I worked for rich - I had lost my way.

Until I found myself traveling to work one morning overcome with sadness…travelling back to work after a late night in the office and just 3 hours sleep I felt trapped. I realized at that moment that my choices and the demands of work were sucking the joy out of life and I felt a desperation to make a change.

I wrote a letter to my now wife sharing the feeling of desperation and dismay that I knew what I wanted in life, but had somehow managed to create an existence that was nothing like what I had set out to achieve.

By the time I finished writing the letter I had made a decision…I decided that life was going to be different than this, somehow I would undo the decisions I had made, reconnect with the dream that I had lost sight of and take action to make it a reality.

That is when I got serious about using the stock market to start building wealth and reset the course of my life.

And eventually…. Success!

I reconnected with the dream of freedom I had for my life, and the knowledge that stock trading was the vehicle that would make it come true. I just didn't exactly know how because I was losing money in the stock market and my results were very erratic.

I had fumbled around unsuccessfully in the stock market for

years doing what my parents did, what my friends did and following the advice of various gurus. My first few years up to this moment were frustrating and unprofitable.

You see, up until that point I had been trying to approach the markets using other people's methods...any my results were terrible:

- I was losing money
- I was impatient
- I was stressed
- I constantly second guessed what I was doing
- I was frustrated!

Trading was the path, and I knew there was money to be made. It's just that I wasn't making any of it!

I was never a trader in a bank or hedge fund, or a prop trader. I was never an investment banker or broker or any of those other unattainable jobs that people associate with successful traders. I did not come from a wealthy family that had all the keys to financial success. At this point all I had was the desire to change my life and be financially free.

My first breakthrough came after really struggling and being almost ready to give up, I came across a series of books that changed the way I looked at making money in the stock markets - they were the Market Wizards books by Jack Schwager.

What I learned reading those 600 or so pages, was that trading is a personal game and that everyone must find an approach that works for them. I also learned that my trading approach has to fit my personality and lifestyle, otherwise there is no chance of me being consistently successful.

I can't make money trading your way, and you can't make money my way… unless you are my long lost twin!

The Market Wizards books are a series of interviews with some of the best traders in the world. As I read each interview, it became obvious that each trader was making a ton of money, was totally comfortable and committed to their own style…and they were all different!

Each interview helped me clarify what did and didn't appeal to me. By the time I got through the Market Wizards books I knew exactly what sort of trader I wanted to be. That was the start of my real journey towards designing my own trading approach that suited me, my objectives and the life I wanted to create.

I had found my trading strategy!

I chose my trading strategy because it is simple, it takes very little time each day to execute, and it has proven the test of time by being consistently profitable for decades!

It took me a lot more effort than it will take you…

Of course this journey was not quite as quick or easy as it sounds…The program I needed (but couldn't find) was a step by step guide to successful trading by helping me to:

1. Understand the language of trading
2. Understand myself enough to choose a strategy that matched my personality, objectives and lifestyle aspirations
3. Formulate, test and get confidence in my trading rules
4. Understand how to manage my risk to meet my objectives
5. Create my trading plan so I knew exactly what to do each day

So in the absence of this guide I found my own way by reading many books and backtesting countless ideas. By the time I managed to formulate and backtest my first trading system I had read over 150 trading books and dedicated countless hours to full time learning and testing of ideas.

All this was required because I didn't have a mentor to guide me nor a community to support me and none of the educators I had come across had a systematic way of showing new traders what to do.

Now I continue to trade essentially the same system I designed way back in 2003 (with a few tweaks and improvements along with way), and it still works as effectively as ever.

My current portfolio of stock trading systems backtest profitably over more than 20 years and have survived all types of markets in real time trading over the last 10 years. This approach to trading is so robust that it works in just about any stock market anywhere in the world. I even tested it on stock indices back as far as 1900…which certainly gave me confidence in my approach!

After that it was onward and upwards, I grew my small account large enough to pay off our home, then set about growing it again to free myself from the workforce. I left the corporate world in 2012 and now spend my time trading, developing new trading systems, educating, speaking and spending time with my wife and kids.

So I have now been consistently profitable for over a decade and make hundreds of thousands of dollars a year working just 20-30 minutes a day trading.

Thankfully (as you will soon see), I have now created exactly the program that I needed way back then, so it won't take you anywhere near as much time and energy as it took me to succeed!

How other trader's pain and hope changed my path…

Now that I had finally 'made it' and was trading successfully and independently, I became increasingly aware of the people around me struggling to do the same thing that I had done.

Slowly more and more people began approaching me for help with their trading. I heard so many stories of struggle, frustration, desperation, loss, fear, bad advice and financial scams. But I also heard stories of hope and the desire for freedom.

These two sides of the same coin created an intense desire for me to share what I had learned, and empower new traders to be independent and profitable

What solidified my commitment to this new mission was when I met someone who had lost their life savings in less than two weeks after handing the money to a broker who had promised huge returns from a managed trading account.

The broker made all the mistakes in the book and cost this person their life savings!

He was devastated…and I was determined. That was when I started developing the program that I wish I had when I started…the result was the Enlightened Stock Trader Development Program. Just like I longed for a decade earlier, this program helps traders:
1. Understand the language of trading
2. Understand their own trading personality and choose a strategy that matches their personality, objectives and lifestyle aspirations
3. Design, formulate, test and get confidence in their trading

rules
4. Understand how to manage their risk to meet their objectives
5. Create their trading plan so they know exactly what to do each day

This step by step approach removes the problem created by most trading educators who teach a single method or set of rules. The problem that the method is the educator's ideal method, not the student's.

The dangerous thing about that is the educator's method is unlikely to fit the student, so the student is unlikely to make money consistently. The student is also dependant on the educator because they were taught a certain method…they were not taught how to develop a method for themselves!

One small change makes all the difference…

Most trading educators teach their specific trading method to their students…regardless of whether it fits the student or not.

I explored this recently by speaking to quite a few traders who had attended other courses…these are some of the comments that were most common:

- "It was really great, but I got lost part way through"
- "I loved the course, but I am still paper trading"
- "I learned a lot, but it really wasn't for me"
- "I tried it for a while but I am not doing it anymore"

These sorts of comments are symptomatic of the method not fitting the student. There are of course students who do 'click' with the method the educator teaches and these are the success stories…but there are a lot of students who walk away without taking consistent action because the method just doesn't suit them.

I believe the significant distinction that makes my approach to teaching stock trading different to just about every other trading educator is that my students learn how to build a trading system (set of rules) that fits their personality, objectives and ideal lifestyle.

My student's don't just learn one trading approach or system; they learn how to build a trading system. The great thing about that is they are independent. They can design a profitable approach that works for them and they also have the skills to design other trading systems for themselves.

*In short…I don't give you a fish,
I teach you how to fish for yourself!*

So the problem I solve for my clients is that I get them past the point of dependence on their trading educator and show them how to be completely independent and empower them with the skills to continue to improve their trading by developing their own trading systems into the future.

Not only does this ensure my clients learn to trade in a way that works for them, but it removes the barriers to trading consistently and virtually eliminates stress from the trading process. The final benefit of learning to trade systematically like this is it dramatically reduces the amount of time you need to spend trading…without reducing your profit potential.

Who does this systematic approach work for?

I have used this approach to teach students from all walks of life – engineers, graphic designers, stay home mums, aged care workers and economists amongst others. All my graduates have developed their own unique stock trading systems, and all of them have confidence in their approach and have hope for the future.

The key distinction that makes new traders successful is the willingness to take personal accountability and the desire to succeed.

Like any worthwhile endeavour, learning to trade stocks profitably takes some effort…But the great thing about the Enlightened Stock Trader Development Program is the amount of effort and uncertainty has been dramatically reduced for you. It also helps if you are not afraid of computers and have some basic math capabilities to fall back on (we are talking about money and trading here after all!)

As a new trader you no longer have to take the multi year journey that I took – in just 4 months you could learn how to build a profitable stock trading system that uniquely fits you!

From there trading with real money becomes an easy and natural step.

Enabling transformation, hope, confidence & freedom

When taking new traders through this process there are several critical moments that I really love and I see them almost every time I take a new client on.

When you take the Enlightened Stock Trader Development program, these are the moments that I live for…

The moment you dare to dream big and forget about 'normal' or 'reasonable' life goals

The moment you open yourself to 'real' conversations about money

The moment you leave behind your
stress and 'baggage' about money

The moment your fear of
the stock market evaporates

The moment the quality of your questions
shifts from uncertain to insightful

The moment of joy when your
system idea backtests profitably

The moment of pride when you share your final
system rules with me and they fit you perfectly

The moment of confidence when you take your first trade according to your
trading system and written trading plan

I have had all of these moments with my students, and this is what keeps me passionate and motivated to educate. The personal transformation and growth that comes with learning to trade is what I love…and yes the money is good to…but as you will soon learn, it is about so much more than just the money!

Life is about more than just trading…it is about growth

Outside of trading and teaching trading, I spend a lot of time with my wife and kids and I also spend a lot of time on my own personal development and learning. I really resonate with a phase that T Harv Eker commonly uses "If you are not growing you are dying".

Growth and transformation is something that I crave in all areas of my life, and I sincerely believe that this not only improves my personal life, but my trading and my ability to teach as well. Continuous growth in myself, my relationships and my business is hugely important to me…in the last few years I have been to a huge number of programs to feed this craving for growth.

As you can probably imagine it was a great source of pride for me when my kids went off to their first 'Supercamp', which is an outstanding personal development, life and learning skills program for kids. Both of my young kids (aged 7 and 9) are programming their own games for the iPad and have already written their first webpage - with a little tech support from dad. They are also just about ready to start trading their own accounts - also with a little guidance from dad.

So the kids are on the growth path too which I just love!

Creating this environment of growth for myself and my relationship with my wife and my family is very important to me. Trading is a perfect complement to this and teaching stock trading has allowed me to extend this passion to my students as well.

I hope you will join me on this journey too!

So what's next…

My dream is to leave a legacy of permanent change in the trading and financial education industry.

This change will empower traders globally to have a true understanding of the principles of profitable stock trading. It will improve the quality of life and bring freedom to traders and their families all over the world as well as dramatically reducing the number of people falling victim to poor money management and investment scams.

If this journey resonates with you and sounds like something you are interested in pursuing then go to http://www.enlightenedstocktrading.com/about/ and enter your name and email to find out more about the Enlightened Stock Trader Development program – I guarantee you won't regret it!

Trade Profitably

Adrian Reid

Founder – Enlightened Stock Trading

Adrian Reid

Adrian is a private trader, as well as the founder and Trading Coach at Enlightened Stock Trading (www.enlightenedstocktrading.com) which is dedicated to educating and supporting traders on their journey to profitable systems trading.

Adrian started regularly trading stocks around 13 years ago having been interested in the stock market ever since playing the "Stock Market Game" as a kid of 9 with his family. He now trades stocks privately for his own family account using a portfolio of medium-long term mechanical trading systems.

He trades long / short across Australian and international stock markets. Adrian's trading systems have consistently outperformed international share markets with dramatically reduced risk over the past 10 years.

Adrian left the corporate world in 2012 after making hundreds of thousands of dollars a year working just 30 minutes a day managing his trading systems. This was in stark contrast to the 12-15 hours a day he was spending on his corporate job while earning less money!

Adrian's systematic approach to stock trading generates both income and wealth creation which allows him to spend the majority of his time with his wife Stephanie and three children (Makayla – 15, Quinlan – 9 and Arielle 6). He is also an avid student of personal development, having studied programs by Tony Robbins, Blair Singer, Brendon Burchard, T. Harv Ecker, Van Tharp and many others.

Educating traders is a passion of Adrian's having been infuriated by the scams and misinformation in the trading industry. Adrian started Enlightened Stock Trading to educate traders in the principles of profitable independent trading. Adrian is focused on empowering stock traders – teaching you to be independently successful rather than relying on him for advice like most educators.

Through Enlightened Stock Trading, Adrian's goal is to help you achieve financial freedom and your ideal lifestyle sooner by building your own unique trading system which suits your objectives, personality and ideal lifestyle.

Adrian is the creator of the 'Enlightened Stock Trader Development Program'. This program transforms novice traders into accomplished systematic stock traders in just 4 months. He achieves this by:
Teaching you the language of stock trading and trading systems
Helping you discover your unique trading personality with his T6 Trader Profile
Sharing his unique process for developing profitable trading systems
Showing you how to manage your risk and portfolio to meet

your objectives

Helping you develop your own professional trading plan

Adrian is passionate about sharing the principles of profitable stock trading and helping new traders grow. He is a Blair Singer Training Academy Certified Trainer ensuring your trading education is a transformational experience and he works daily with groups of traders and individuals to build their capability and expertise.

For a Free Report on the Principles of Enlightened and Profitable Stock Trading, opt in at www.enlightenedstocktrading.com

Connect with Adrian to learn more:
LinkedIn: https://sg.linkedin.com/in/adrianjreid
Facebook: www.facebook.com/enlightenedstocktrading
Web: www.enlightenedstocktrading.com
YouTube: https://www.youtube.com/channel/UCDSJ8VRoAUiLK_SJ7OeCahg

12

A FASTER WAY TO CREATE THE RESULTS YOU WANT IN LIFE & BUSINESS...WITH THE FA²ST SYSTEM™

- BY GLENN DIETZEL, BUSINESS MENTOR TO THE WORLD'S HIGHEST PAID BUSINESS COACHES, CONSULTANTS, EXPERTS AND ADVISORS

Yes, you have a big dream! In order to access your big dream, and actually make it a reality in your life, you need to create legacy-building confidence.

What I am about to share, I've really never heard anybody speak about before. It comes from my life experiences and from being deeply involved in other people's lives on a daily basis...especially my fantastic clients all over the world!

This chapter is about becoming 'the person you must become.'

What does "legacy building confidence" mean? It means you develop enough self-assurance to move forward every day toward making your dreams a reality. It also means acquiring the attitudes, skills and knowledge necessary to make your dream happen. But developing legacy building confidence isn't all about you or your success. It's not about what you do for people, it's about how you can leave a lasting impression in the lives you touch.

Yes, most important of all, creating legacy-building confidence means having the opportunity to leave a gift in the lives you touch every day. How do you leave this legacy in people? As I mentioned, it all begins with being the person you must become.

When you have a powerful dream, it's because you are meant to take action on it. Naturally, you can't do it alone. You need to surround yourself with people who will help you move forward, and at the same time prevent you from remaining 'status-quo'.

You need guidance. You need mentors to show you the way.

Becoming the person you must become comes down to a number of key principles. The following is part of the mentoring that I do to assist people from all over the world to accomplish the following: 1. start and grow an 'advice based business'; 2. and stand apart confidently in a 'sea of sameness' so they can achieve their life's calling--their legacy.

I want to share with you how to create what I refer to as the 'fast' approach to change so that you can build confidence to go for your BIG DREAM.

Before I explain the system, let me tell you this. It's powerful, its proprietary, and I guarantee you it absolutely works. I have used it myself over and over again, and I have taught others how to use it to break free from their self-imposed limitations, and set themselves on an accelerated path to success.

Let me explain some principles about change, and some basic premises before I teach you how to change any behavior quickly. When you can do this repeatedly, you can begin to go after your dream and the goals you have for yourself and your life.

Consider the following:

Major premise: "I can control my thoughts."

If you don't think you can control your thoughts, then you need some help. You can control your thoughts. You are a responsible human being. Your thoughts don't have to run rampant in your mind. You can and you must learn to take charge of your thoughts, and teach yourself to have more control.

Action: I control my thoughts.

Minor premise: "My feelings come from my thoughts."

Like thoughts, emotions do not have to act like demanding toddlers who always get their way. You can and must take charge of your emotions. Don't let them force you into bad decisions, and never ever let them coax you into giving up on your big dream.

Action: I am not my emotions. I choose to control my emotions.

Conclusion: "I can control my feelings by controlling my thoughts."

I can remember so many times in my past where I didn't do

something that I knew would bring me closer to my dream just because I 'lost' the feeling. Perhaps you can relate. You have a feeling late at night before you go to bed that you can do anything, but by seven the following morning you have lost this feeling of confidence. ARG!

For many years this kind of pattern had a debilitating effect on my actions and results. My limiting beliefs stopped me for years from launching my own business. The problem was quite simple: I let my feelings and fear control me. It's still painful to consider how much time I lost!

The quickest way to control your feelings is to take action. Here are three simple steps to consider: 1. Make a decision; 2. Build a new belief; and 3. Reinforce that new belief with action. You can't sit and try to out-think fear because fear will always win.

Once you understand the major and minor premises stated above, you will want to put them into practice. This will require you to become more aware of your prevailing thoughts and feelings so you can make changes as necessary.

Which brings me to another one of my favorite topics: Change.

Glenn Dietzel's Three Pillars of Change

1. **Change is personal: "I need to change."**

Change is intensely personal and you'll never embark on any major goal or lifestyle change or dream until you understand that you need to change, and feel it deeply.

2. **Change is possible: "I am able to change."**

If you don't think it's possible for you to make a change, it will never happen. Your expectations create your experience. Believe that you can change. Will it be difficult? Of course it will! But believe it is possible and miraculously, you will enjoy the process.

3. **Change is profitable: "I will be rewarded for change."**

Now I'm not talking about financial or other tangible rewards, although those will certainly come to you as you become the person you must become. What I'm talking about here are the intangible rewards for change, and these are the most motivating ones. The increased confidence, the increased self-esteem, the increased power of believing in yourself which you will experience, as a by-product, will bring a world of opportunity and countless other rewards into your life. That I can promise you!

When You Change Your Thinking, You Change Your Beliefs

John Maxwell put this very well. "A belief is not just an idea you possess; it is an idea that possesses you." What this means is that ideas are not the same as beliefs. Ideas come and go, and some change your life and others don't. But beliefs are the ideas that have such a firm hold on your mind and on your life that they guide all your thoughts and actions. That's what beliefs do. They direct every thought you have and every action you take. That's why beliefs are so powerful.

Attitude Determines Action

The psychologist William James wrote, "That which holds our attention determines our action." What we focus on creates our attitudes, and attitudes drive action. When you believe differently you will think differently and then you will act differently.

Do you have it in you to change your thoughts and your beliefs, and thus change how you act? Are you focused enough and powerful enough to make your big dream a reality? I know you have it in you to change, but YOU have to know it too. You have to expect nothing but the best from yourself and know, beyond any shadow of a doubt, that you can succeed.

Whatever you believe is true for you will be true. In other words, if you believe you will fail, you will fail. Conversely, if you believe you will win, you will win!

OK, let's get to work. Let's give you the tool for change you need. I want you to write down FA²ST™. It's really F-A-A-S-T, with two A's, but I write it as A-squared for a powerful reason. The process is not linear—it's not a straight line at all. It has a velocity component creating geometric—or accelerated—growth. My clients do not want linear growth, they want fast-tracked growth hence the reason I use the A-squared.

Important Principles of the FA²ST System

We all want to change things quickly, right?

Super successful people are able to make key changes in their behavior literally on the fly.

This is especially important in business which is near and dear to my heart.

Because of the realities in today's ever changing world, the most successful CEOs and entrepreneurs are the ones that can adapt to change the quickest.

Most people think change is difficult.

Yes, change can be uncomfortable, but it doesn't have to be difficult if you use a system to assist you.

I personally believe you can make fast changes. In fact, I might be going out on a limb to say this, but I believe anyone can make profound changes in their lives if they use a proven system.

With the FA²ST system, you can change any behavior you want in as little as five minutes, and I'm going to show you how to do that. Any behavior at all! If you are to become the person you must become, you need to have a system to help you.

What needs to happen is this: You need to start telling yourself a new story—one that empowers you to achieve the greatness within you—one that launches you toward being the person you must become. Get ready because you are about to learn how to change your personal story. You are about to revolutionize your life, quickly and easily. Isn't that exciting?

Now to change that story, it comes down to constructing new behaviors. You need to drop the old ways of acting which are not giving you the results you want, and start with brand new behaviors. In order to do that, you must understand something else about how the brain works, and how habits become entrenched into your way of thinking and behaving.

Science shows us that once a behavior is established, it is literally hard-wired into your brain. The brain cells (neurons) are a basic part of your thinking.

Your decision to make a change starts as a thought. When you have the same thought over time, it becomes a thought pattern. When you keep practicing the new way of thinking and acting, you make it stronger and it becomes a new habit. Literally you develop new neural pathways! Isn't that amazing?

The Subconscious Mind at Work

Why do I refer to the subconscious mind? It's because this is the part of your brain which is actually doing the thinking most of the time. It's been programmed through years and years of history. You have inadvertently trained your subconscious mind to work against you by internalizing other people's stories about your life, many of them probably holding you hostage to your big dream right now.

The subconscious mind is controlled to a large degree by the reticular activating system or RAS. What's that you might ask? It's the part of the brain responsible for goal setting. It's the part of your brain that controls what you see yourself capable of accomplishing. More importantly, when you retrain your RAS it will harness the power of expectation and help you realize your true potential for you to be the person you must become.

Your RAS is always on the alert to reaffirm the story you have about success. In order to change your story, you must realize that your current story playing over and over again in your subconscious must be re-orchestrated.

Your mind is constantly asking you questions. It's doing this all the time, and it's doing it right now! The sad thing is that most of the time it's asking the same mind-limiting, life-inhibiting questions day after day after day. This is why it's so important to learn how to talk to yourself so you can change.

A 'Speed-to-Market' principle I teach to all my clients is, 'Writing is the doing part of thinking.' The fastest way to create a new set of questions and answers for your brain, and create deeper levels of concentration, is to begin to physically write things down. Writing is literally the most kinesthetic way of activating your subconscious allowing you to begin re-programming new beliefs about what you can achieve. This is also very instrumental in setting new goals.

This is why I encourage you to write, because when you are done writing and go back to doing what you were doing, your subconscious mind is now working on the answers to your questions. It's processing and coming up with answers for you without you consciously thinking about solutions. Your subconscious is refocusing and rechanneling your thoughts on the fly! How powerful is that!

Introducing the FA²ST™ System

This innovative technique will revolutionize your life—and your business—as you set and accomplish more empowering goals for yourself.

"F" is for Focus

You have to focus on what you want in life and analyze the limiting beliefs you have established. Your current beliefs are represented by your current actions. Begin to focus on new beliefs which you want to realize as new behaviors in your life. Your beliefs drive your actions. It's ultimately why you do what you're doing, and it's based on the values that you have.

Analyze the questions that you're asking in the back of your mind, and learn to ask yourself more powerful questions which will move you forward. And of course, you should write these down, because you know that: "Writing is the doing part of thinking!"

Now focus on new and more powerful questions. Ask these questions in an emotionally charged way. In other words, formulate these questions in a way which connects you to them emotionally. Do to yourself what salespeople and marketers do to you all the time. Play to your own emotions. Draw on their power.

For example, tell yourself a new story about why you deserve success. Focus on the new belief system. Instead of asking yourself, "Why me?"—reframe the question into, "Why not me?" Say it over and over again, and connect to this more empowering question with greater emotion.

Thomas Fuller, chaplain to King Charles II of England, said, "He that is everywhere is nowhere." In other words, without focus, you cannot succeed.

Your success and your legacy start with focus. Concentrate on the following:
1. A new belief;
2. A better question; and
3. A more powerful answer.

When you input better questions into your brain, you will begin to get better answers! This is a great way of empowering your thinking. When you do this successfully, watch your life begin to change quickly.

OK, so that's focus. Now what about the first A?

The First "A" is for Action

As you reprogram your thinking with new beliefs about what's possible for your life, what specific actions are you going to take?

The quickest way of reinforcing new beliefs and thoughts you're developing is to take action. Unfortunately, it's not good enough to decide what needs to change. You need to DO something, take action on it to reinforce the decision and belief.

Now I want to give you an example from my own life, then I want to challenge you to commit to changing yours. Let's use the idea of speaking, because that was a major hurdle for me to overcome.

For years I said to myself, "Who am I to speak in front of tens of thousands of people?" This question was killing any opportunity for me to actually realize goals and dreams because I was asking the wrong question.

It was fear based.

So I reprogrammed the question to the following: "Why not me to speak in front of ten thousand people?" The change is subtle, but it had a profound impact on developing a new belief within me about speaking and success. As well, the emotion that it created within me propelled me forward with my new, more empowering belief.

I knew I could confidently speak in front of ten thousand people because to be the person I must become, would require me to get over this limitation so I would be able to confidently share my story and message with the world.

It's your turn. I know there's something you're good at, and I know someone at work or church or in a community organization will ask you to share and teach that skill. So here's what you do.

Write this down...

"The next time somebody says I'm good at _____, I am going to take action and accept the challenge." If you aren't comfortable with the way I put it, simply use whatever words fit your personality and situation.

The key is to write down the situation, and the specific actions you are going to take. The first step is to accept the challenge—the new belief.

When you accept a challenge despite the doubt or uncertainty you feel, this means taking action. That's how you edify or strengthen the new belief, and make it work in your life.

That's Action. What's the second A for??

The Second "A" is for Accountability

A promise made alone is soon broken. You need other people in your life to hold you accountable. You need to share what you really want in life and where you want to go; but be careful! You can't just blab your dreams and your deepest desires to anyone. You need to share your dreams with people who will really help you move forward, such as mentors and coaches.

If you are to achieve the success you want, and be the person you must become, you need to be accountable to someone outside yourself.

One of my accountability partners has been my wife, Fiona. She checked in on me with respect to how I was doing when I first decided to go for my big dream, and how I was reacting to various situations. She also made certain to ask if I were doing my journaling. She was hugely supportive, and I am still thankful for her love and encouragement. You have to be accountable for your life in order to be the person you must become.

Now it's your turn. Who do you have in your life that will hold you accountable – that will help you grow as a person and not "sugar coat" what you honestly need to hear? Maybe you have someone like Fiona, and your spouse will be your best and truest ally. Maybe it's someone else. Write about it in your journal. Then talk to this person and explain what you need. Arrange to check in every week—or better yet, every day.

You have discovered the power of accountability in your life. So now what? Here's the next piece.

"ST" is for Self-Talk

Finally, the "ST" stands for self-talk or mental follow-through.

You've focused on what you want; you've taken the necessary action; you've found somebody to be accountable to in order to make sure you're taking action. Now, you've got to have the proper Self Talk, because you will not get the results you want every time. There are going to be disappointments. There are going to be setbacks. Success is not easy. If it were, everybody would be living their big dream.

How do I know that most people are not? Well, just listen to the talk that goes on in the lunchroom at work—or listen to any average conversation. People are always wishing they were living someone else's life.

Here's another example from my own life. It's like shooting a jump shot. I'm a basketball junky, and I used to coach when I was a teacher. There's a lot to think about when you shoot a jump-shot. Shooting that basket comes from facing the hoop head-on, having the right stance and co-ordinating your body to move from your feet to your fingers in a finely-tuned effort to successfully score a basket.

But that's just the beginning. Shooting success ultimately comes down to the follow-through. As I would tell students when I was coaching, "It's like waving to grandma. You have to wave good-bye to grandma after the ball leaves your hands."

Now that might seem like a silly example, but I want you to understand that the follow through is key in every new behavior you undertake to achieve new goals for your life.

With the basketball example I just presented, you probably understand this already, but just to be clear—you're not always going to make the basket. Sometimes you're going to miss. What goes on inside your head after that miss is hugely important. Proper self-talk afterwards means knowing that if you don't reach your goal this time, you will make it next time. Proper self-talk means saying, "I'm better than that, and next time I'll make it!"

Goal setting needs to be flexible. You need to realize that you are not always going to achieve your goal the first time. But this doesn't mean you should never set goals.

As the saying goes, "How do you eat an elephant?" One bite at a time, of course! Getting where you want to go is just a series of small mini-steps so that you come closer and closer to your ultimate destination.

I want you to take action right now. Don't bypass this step. Reward yourself with positive self-talk when you succeed. When you miss, you have feedback ready. Program yourself ahead of time for success.

Now it's your turn. Plan and write down what you're going to say to yourself when you succeed, and what you're going to say to yourself when you miss the mark. Plan ahead. Then when the situation arises, you'll be well prepared to move toward success, even if you don't achieve the results you wanted the first time.

In Summary

By following the FA²ST system you will be able to make faster change in your life and business.

You will finally be able to optimize your behavior and achieve the results that you want.

It all starts with new beliefs.

Before you know it, the new beliefs you have practiced will be as solid and sturdy as the old path. You're going to be hard-wired for success. You will be living a life of possibilities—and you will truly be the person you must become...

GLENN DIETZEL

Glenn Dietzel is an internationally recognized Thought Leader and business acceleration strategist. Glenn has created a revolutionary business approach to creating, selling and scaling the value of your advice quickly and easily. His high velocity growth strategies are used by business leaders globally allowing them to command maximum fees and royalties.

Are you ready to engineer Speed-to-Market Success? Companies who want results-driven training to achieve pre-eminence in their market turn to Glenn Dietzel, a teacher by passion and profession and an internationally recognized Thought Leader and high-performance business strategist specializing in execution. Glenn's breakthrough strategies inspire, educate and empower entrepreneurial CEOs and leadership teams globally.

From two US Presidential consultants to leaders across dozens of industries, many refer to Glenn as their 'unfair competitive advantage' leaning on his advice to stand apart. His clients and strategic alliance partners have been able to transact over $250 million in added revenue after integrating both education-based and value-based selling systems.

Over the past several years Glenn has ventured 'behind-the-scenes' assisting corporations and business leaders to co-brand his systems as he consults them with their growth opportunities. Glenn's unique approach to growing and scaling companies allows his clients to use the hundreds of systems, tools, blueprints, and business accelerators he has created over the past 13+ years so they also command maximum fees for coaching, training, and keynoting as an expert advisor in their market

Glenn is also the co-founder of Expert Advisor Alliance. A new platform to bring top industry experts together for collaboration, partnerships and royalties through licensing, certification and co-branding so they can grow their exposure and influence in an over-crowded market place. Glenn's mission is to create a new standard of professional growth while fostering a love of business for tomorrow's entrepreneurial leaders. In his down time Glenn loves travelling to Scotland with his family.

SHASHIDHAR JAKKALI

13

YOUR MILLION DOLLAR MAGNIFICENT MESSAGE HOW TO CREATE DEMAND FOR YOURSELF AS A HIGHLY PAID SPEAKER, PRESENTER OR CONSULTANT EVEN IF YOU DON'T THINK YOU'RE AN EXPERT!

- BY CYDNEY O' SULLIVAN, CEO, MILLIONAIRES ACADEMY

I have been building businesses for a very long time, over 30 years, in fact I was a major shareholder in one of the most successful IPO's in Australia. I have developed real estate, traded the stock market and flipped retail businesses. In my life I have experience of earning nearly a billion US dollars worth of business income and I genuinely believe that thanks to modern technologies one of the fastest and most cost-effective ways to create wealth today is building your authority and personal earning power through Speaking, Webinars and Workshops.

Our personal earning power is generally dictated by a number of factors:
- Education
- Experience
- Celebrity
- Talent
- Abilities

But what if you could massively shortcut the journey by focusing on one of your strengths to offer solutions to a market that values and is willing to invest in those solutions? I spent over US$1 million dollars and ten years to learn that if we could just focus our energies to that one goal, it's surprisingly easy to attain expertise and authority.

As a professional marketer and publisher I have helped my clients use almost every tool you could think of to promote their businesses, and the fastest way to create connection and add a lot of income to your business is to get out and meet your customers, prospects and leads. Get out there networking online and offline and show them how much you care about them, offer them your products and programs and watch your business grow. Done right, it's magic, and it's fun!

I'm going to share with you how to use your knowledge and life experience for positioning so that your ideal clients start seeking YOU out, and FINDING you.

I'm going to share the success formula that I have been

teaching my high paying clients to help them get clarity and business success, and what I've seen work over and over in a variety of industries. I'll share what's helped us generate millions in new sales over the last 4 years, when everyone else was telling us there was a recession.

Would you agree that writing a professional book full of great advice that showcases you as an expert in your field will help establish you as a more credible and authoritative choice over your competition who hasn't?

Did you know that writing even a short book can give you fantastic clarity about your expertise and help share it with others? The secret is that when you back such a book up with a great website, strong social and traditional media presence, and public speaking that it's an absolutely winning combination for success. I have assisted many experts to use this combination to make hundreds of thousands to even millions of dollars.

The STARS™ Success Formula

The formula is made up of five components and it's important to get them in the right order. Implementing them in the wrong order often leads to a massive waste of time, effort and lots of wasted money.

They are:

S-T-A-R-S
1. Strengths – Play to yours
2. Tribe – Know your market
3. Authority – Establish your expertise
4. Reach – Expand your exposure
5. Scale – Build with systems and promotion

Once you know how to fill or speak at an event with the right audience, make an attractive offer that is of genuine value to some of the people in the audience and process your orders efficiently, then deliver on your sales promises, you can literally earn tens of thousands to millions of dollars per event.

If you don't want to run your own events, but become an accomplished speaker who is able to create demand and close sales, you can make an equally impressive fortune speaking at other people's organisations, events, seminars, webinars, teleseminars, certification programs, and trainings. That's just a few of the places that you can find opportunities to practice sales presentations. There are also Chambers of Commerce, Community Centers, Libraries, Networking events, and you're only limited by your own ability to market yourself and grow.

From Tragedy to Triumph

On May 3rd, 1980, 13 year old Cari Lightner was hit by a car while walking to a church carnival with a friend. She was struck with such force that she was knocked out of her shoes and thrown 125 feet. The driver that hit Cari was drunk and never even stopped. After the police told Cari's mother Candy that the driver likely would receive little punishment for taking the life of her daughter, Candy became enraged.

She decided to channel her anger and grief into fighting drunk driving. Four days after Cari's death, Candy Lightner started a grassroots organization to advocate for stiffer penalties for drunk driving. That became Mothers Against Drunk Drivers.

Before starting MADD, Candy hadn't been involved in social reform or politics, but she proved to be a tireless fighter and was able to get laws changed all over the USA.

The Foundational Pillars of the STARSTM Formula

It all starts with these 5 easy to remember steps:

S is for Strengths

What are yours? What do you love to do, who do you love to serve and support? Play to your strengths, and seek out others who are great at covering your weaknesses. When you focus on being your most effective and extraordinary it's far more powerful than trying to make yourself better at things you don't like.

In the speaking and training business knowing your strengths, and using those to advantage you can position yourself for success. This can be an absolute game changer.

1. To position yourself effectively as a leader in your area of expertise you should research your market and take the time to know your customer's needs, pains and pleasure points.

2. Understand the importance of and make the investment in developing a professional brand, bio and marketing message.

3. Seek out and invest in relationships with influencers and your marketplace and create alliances to faster leverage your credibility and open doors.

T is for your Tribe

Once you are clear on your strengths, unique offering and

positioning, THAT is when successful businesses research and really get to know their ideal target market and the influencers in that market.

1. Craft and practice your unique script to engage audiences and separate yourself from the competition

2. Create offers and products specifically tailored to your ideal market, they should feel highly valuable, irresistible and desirable.

3. Invest in automated marketing campaigns that lead your audiences to offers that are relevant to their needs and problems.

Who do you want to work with? Who does it most please you to serve? Who will be your support network? There are billions of people in the world, you're not a fit for all of them. Platforms like Google, Facebook and Instagram allow you to do a lot of demographic and psychographic targeting and research. The clearer you are on whom you can best serve, and who can really best serve you, the more easily you put yourself where they are.

From Misfit to Master of Business
Billionaire Richard Branson started his first business at the age of sixteen, a magazine called Student. By the age of 22, he had opened a chain of record stores, and he is now best known as the founder of Virgin Group, which encompasses more than 400 companies. He has dyslexia and his poor academic performance prompted his headmaster to tell him he would either end up in prison or become a millionaire.

The A is your Authority

Once you know who your "Public" self will be, and whom you can best serve, the more easily you'll find it to build your authority and credibility. With a book or two, some well crafted presentations and the appropriate social or media channels, you can soon establish your authority, and you'll be surprised, that will be enough. Most people get stuck, so if you step up with authority, they assume and accept that you are one. Our clients who come from an academic background find this very hard to swallow, but the world is full of living examples of passionate people with little formal education who are making a huge difference in the world.

I see so many businesses pouring money into paid promotions when they don't even have their positioning and marketing campaigns in place. This can drain your finances, distract your focus and ultimately hurt your business.

1. Set up authoritative web presences to collect prospect contact information so you can build relationships and referral communities
2. Use marketing and media to get access to major distribution networks
3. Use cutting edge technologies like social media marketing, video marketing, and webinars for greater reach and competitive edge.

All the while developing your automated systems…

From Desperation to Inspiration

Nick Vujicic, is an Australian motivational speaker born with Tetra-amelia syndrome, he was born without arms or legs. As a child, he struggled mentally and emotionally, as well as physically, but eventually came to terms with his disability and, at the age of seventeen, started his own non-profit organization, Life Without Limbs. Nick is now an inspirational speaker worldwide, who shares about hope, and finding meaning in life. He has now inspired millions of people and is happily married with a young family.

The R is for Reach & Revenue

The next part of the formula is to promote your authority in a way that is leveraged, efficient and profitable. Coming from a lifetime of building businesses, and having worked with so many wonderful, passionate people whose progress was continuously bottlenecked by their lack of funding, I believe you should also have a plan to create automated wealth built-in to give you support, security and celebration as you grow.

This is one of the most exciting aspects of marketing in business today thanks to the internet and all the promotional mediums available to us today. But it's also an area that so many businesses are not even fully aware of.

1. Successful businesses have simple systems that control the client experience from the first sales contact through to a paid product or service and even the after-sales experiences
2. Have simple sales processes that make it easy to take

prospects to clients
3. Maximize the results of their marketing efforts and collect the revenues in the most automated and leveraged way possible, always reviewing and improving on their systems and customer experience.

And finally the S is for Scale and Systems

Automating the whole process so that you can step out of the administration and be in your greatest creative flow.

Stepping into your star power to become an inspirational leader is just like any other business growth decision. It should be profitable and rewarding.

Thanks to modern technologies even very small businesses can have professional processes now that allow them to process large orders and lots of sales. It's not unusual for well-organized speakers today to process hundreds of thousands of dollars in orders at a single event. They can take the annual revenue of most small to medium sized businesses in a few hours!

So where do you start implementing the STARSTM formula to build your celebrity and authority?

1. Choose Your Leadership Position

Choose your niche and topic of expertise

Your qualifications, life experience or passionate interests will largely determine what particular niche you choose to plant your stake in and call your own. But, if you're smart, you'll also take into consideration market demand, how 'cashed up' a market sector is and the competition.

Also research your local market and global market to find out who you are competing with in that category.

Keep it Simple!!

Don't overcomplicate this process. This is where I see most inexperienced people wasting effort, time and money – making things much more complicated than they need to be.

Is there another person doing a great job with their positioning you could model? Who do you think their target market is and how are they talking the language of that customer base?

2. Create A Game Plan

At this stage you need a game plan that shows you understand your market, you've worked out the numbers, worked out the best marketing strategies, and delivery options so you can know when you'll hit your revenue targets. If you don't hit your targets, you'll be able to adjust the plan and know where you went wrong and correct the plan. Then you can leverage your sales and marketing funnels to allow you growth.

Shortcuts

Once you're executing your plan, there are plenty of shortcuts – outsourcing, modeling, and technology. These are advanced topics and I could write a book on each of these! Don't let these be distractions and delay your forward momentum.

If you hire others to help where you are inexperienced or to manage areas that are not your strength it should pay off in speed to market. But be careful, finding genuine support in this industry is a bit of a minefield. Check out any service providers and support teams extensively. Do your due diligence.

3. Write The Presentation To Get Clear On The Message

Now it's time to write your presentation. Here is what we advise most strongly:

1. Create Your Presentation
2. Test it to small audiences (webcast or small group of friends) before going live, practice, tweak and present again
3. Test present again to a small, friendly live audience and incorporate valid and qualified feedback
4. Test your presentation on another audience and incorporate valid and qualified feedback
5. Practice, practice, practice

What Makes a Good Speech – Crafting the Presentation

There are as many ways to give a speech as there are topics, audiences, and different kinds of people in the world. There are inspirational speeches, entertaining presentations, keynotes, educational and sales presentations to name just a few of the different styles.

For the purposes of this book I'll focus on a combination of styles that is designed to engage the interest of the audience, invoke an emotional connection and create a desire in as many as possible that leads to them deciding to move forward with you in some way towards a commercial outcome.

Your speech should be entertaining, engaging, inspiring, authentic and paced so that your audience come on a journey with you. There are a number of well established techniques that you can incorporate into your presentation that encourage your audience to interact with, and feel more connected and trusting towards you. These can be learned in our advanced trainings, and they are very powerful.

4. Establishing Your Expertise

Once you have your presentation and are clear on the area of expertise where you are going out to market, it's time to start building up your expert credibility.

Here are some tips to get you started:

- Social proof – any awards, special achievements, client endorsements, well-known companies you've worked for or with, big name clients who don't mind you using their names on your websites and brochures

- Case studies – showcase your successes and those of your clients

- Testimonials – ask high profile people you've worked with to give you an endorsement or testimonial in writing, audio or video form. If you have audio or video it's easy to transcribe to written. Also get testimonials from your clients and customers. Think creatively, for instance even your suppliers might like to give you testimonials.

- Media and Published Credibility – if you've had any books published, articles, been featured in the newspaper, on the radio or on TV, consider adding these to your website and marketing.

- Speaking Engagements – if you've spoken with other big

name speakers, or if you've spoken at big events. These can also be mentioned in your marketing collateral.

- Even if you don't have any of these things, now is the time to start getting them organized, and to find out how you can make this happen come over and join our free trainings at https://MillionairesAcademy.com to see how surprisingly easy it is to put steps in motion to build your own authority positioning.

Marketing Online

Marketing online has become one of the most cost-effective and results-effective ways to launch a business quickly and profitably in today's market.

- Build a professional business site that showcases your business and speaking programs that is search engine optimized to the terms people would use to find you as a solution provider or speaker in your niche.

- Use Social Media platforms to appear professional; in particular Linkedin, Facebook, Google+, Instagram, Twitter and Pinterest.

Don't Be Cheap on Your Way to Success!
Remember! Don't be cheap on your branding and websites

Professionals want to work with other professionals and they WILL check you out and they will judge you on ugly, outdated, or cheap looking websites and marketing materials. Invest in your professional image.

5. Products and Programs

What should you sell as a professional speaker?

Firstly, make sure you like delivering what you're selling and want to talk about it and help people on an ongoing basis.

Other People's Products and Services, Training, or Programs

Where most people first get into giving public presentations is either as an educator or trainer or selling for others as part of their job, or often people find out they are a good speaker while promoting network marketing programs.

You Might Prefer to Sell Your Own Programs, Coaching and Trainings

I recommend that once you know your niche and topic you write books about it and that will give you the foundations to create training programs, coaching programs, certification trainings and programs. Or you might prefer to create your consulting, coaching or training program and produce books later, or never at all.

Tips:

- Create your packages in a way that makes it very easy for people to buy
- Make them relevant, market appropriate and competitive

6. Marketing Campaigns – The Magic Formula to Acquire and Nurture leads

Marketing campaigns earlier are magic once effectively planned, built and set in place. This is one of the most important aspects of the success formula, and one of the areas I see most commonly left out or poorly executed. Not setting up marketing campaigns with automated sales funnels is literally leaving most of the cash in your business largely untapped.

The goal of the campaign and subsequent nurturing process is to attract and then convert the leads who show initial interest into prospects, then through a natural filtering process, convert them into customers and raving fans and referral advocates.

7. Set Up Your Delivery Process and Systems

Make sure whatever you sell – you can deliver!

You need to be able to deliver what you market. Few things will hurt your business more than getting your positioning right, your packaging right, your sales working and then failing to deliver on your promise.

Automation and technology

I recommend products and services that can be delivered digitally with all of today's modern technologies. Though with the amazing online retail facilities that are available, it's not hard to deliver physical books and programs through Amazon, eBay and other similar online platforms that have massive audiences and distribution networks in place already.

8. Promotion

Effective Marketing

I recommend you focus on marketing that monetizes along the way. Whether it's starting with free marketing options and seeing what works, or paid advertising – there will be some promotional mediums and strategies that are more effective than others, depending on your topic, niche, offer and target markets.

Getting your marketing right can make the difference between getting in front of 5 people a month and 5000 people a month, and making lots of sales or pouring money down the drain with a fire hose sized tap. With today's technologies **our clients regularly make $50,000 to a $100,000 dollars** from a simple, but strategic, marketing campaign.

If your marketing is not producing **revenue**, it's almost certainly the wrong marketing.

To get help from experienced results-focused professionals with a track record of success, come over to MillionairesAcademy.com and learn from some of the best.

Webcasts & Telecasts

Webcasts and telecasts (also known as podcasts, webinars and teleseminars) are a brilliant and now easily accessible technology to do trainings and presentations online to an audience anywhere in the world. It's easy to set up and manage, and you can host webinars with attendees from all over the world at once! Depending on the platform you choose, you can accommodate an audience of one to thousands. And the cost per broadcast will most likely vary by such factors as the number of attendees, though there are now plenty of free options for broadcasting over the internet.

Social Media

Most people have social media accounts now, such as Facebook and LinkedIn so a great place to start building up a supportive community for your events, speaking engagements and campaigns is by connecting and promoting with social media.

Social media promotional campaigns can be very effective, but do take some time to set up properly and we recommend that this tends to be more of an advanced strategy unless you are a great networker and already have a large following of your target market to promote to.

Emails

Having an effective emailing system in place and crafting engaging emails should be part of your promotional strategy. Then focus on building up your subscriber list every time you go out and speak or network.

9. Sales

Selling

Persuasive influence is what closes the sale, and it's what helps our customers find us, trust us, and how we improve their lives. So we all use it on some level - we just have to get over all the negative hype associated with the word 'sales' - or – on an even deeper level, the resistance and emotional blockages that might be holding you back from asking for money, and pricing your solutions appropriately.

If you are not selling your services or products, then you are not serving the world with your true gifts. You are cheapening your brand and holding back from the industry in which you should be a proud leader and specialist. If you aren't joyfully selling in your business, I'd like to help you get over whatever is holding you back - quickly and seriously. Because you are here reading this book about being ready to step into your authority and destiny, and if you don't get this one thing sorted, all the hard work you put in will come to a bottleneck and hold back your success!

Follow-up: $100,000 or $10,000?

The secret is in the follow up, it's so important and staying in touch can be automated using a well-designed automated sales sequence. With the technology we all have access to today, there is no reason that you cannot do this quite easily and it usually makes a huge financial improvement on the business.

There are great emotional and financial rewards to those who succeed in this industry; wealth, freedom, recognition, and the joy of being able to facilitate the ongoing transformation of yourself and others. Sharing your gifts for financial and spiritual wealth, and being able to help those less fortunate are only some of the rewards of success.

Where you can find Cydney and her team:

I have so much more to teach you! Please visit my website https://MillionairesAcademy.com for your free in-depth step-by-step guide to speaking success and join our community. We regularly hold value packed online trainings.

To Your Great and Fabulous Success!!

Cydney O'Sullivan

Cydney O' Sullivan

Cydney O'Sullivan has been a business 'turn-around' expert most of her life. In her years as a business, real estate and stock market investor she has made millions, and also some costly mistakes, and wants to help you avoid making those in your business and life. She thrives on assisting others achieve their own success as authors and speakers through her business https://MillionairesAcademy.com.

She is a 12 times best-selling business author sharing her own experiences of turning value and service into profit.

Her business advice has been featured in national newspapers and magazines and in many books. She is the founder of several training programs including Millionaires Academy™, Best Seller SuccessTM, Expert Success SummitTM and Social Superstar SecretsTM.

Website: https://MillionairesAcademy.com

SHASHIDHAR JAKKALI

14

ON PARENTING, EDUCATION, AND THE FUTURE

- BY AMI DESAI, CONSCIENTIOUS ENTREPRENEUR AND FOUNDER OF TIERRA LEARNING PYRAMID

The Context:

Social scientists say we are living amidst a generation of millennials. Millennials are those that came of age around the year 2000 or later, or those born in or after 1984. What characterizes millennials? While it is difficult to stereotype such a large set of individuals, broadly these are young adults (aged 13-30 now) who are often identified as being tough to manage, self-interested, unfocussed, lazy, ungrateful, and having a deep sense of entitlement. Sure, we have had such people in the past too. But we never had an entire generation in the past that largely conformed to those characteristics.

https://ucminnovativepr.files.wordpress.com/2014/09/millennial-pic.png

Do you find millennials around you:

- iPhones and such material possessions have become synonymous with identity.

- Chatting on phone takes precedence over talking to a person sitting in front of them.

- Changing of jobs, even careers, every few months or years, is usual.

- Complaining and showing resentment towards parents, lovers, employer, politicians – almost everyone, is a norm.

- From getting into a line to pay a bill or booking a cab to travel to another place, they have lost all patience.

As these children come of age and get ready to take charge of the world, does it make you a little bit nervous or worried? Do you think these young adults have the foundation to make a good life for themselves and to deal with the crisis this fast growing and globally connect world will throw at them? I have my doubts.

I wonder where we went wrong? How did we end up being parents, friends, and employers to a generation we call millennials? Experts identify parenting and education as the major factor for this.

As a mother, a counselor, an educator and an image consultant, I have had the opportunity of looking at lives of children, young adults, grown-ups and even old men and women at close quarters. And the study of these lives has helped me refine my ideas of parenting and education. Through this small essay, drawing from experiences of my own life, I'd make an attempt to propose some reasons why we are surrounded by millennials, and how we can possibly reverse this trend.

My Journey:

Born and brought up in Mumbai (then Bombay) to a family of Gujarati businessmen but a scientist grandfather, I had inclination towards both sciences and human behavior. I did my studies in Statistics, but as was the norm of the time, soon got married and moved to Bangalore.

Moving to Bangalore from Mumbai was a real cultural shock, both in and out of house. Inside, transitioning from a daughter to a daughter-in-law was complicated. Outside, getting used to a quite, calm, no-body-on-streets sort of Bangalore was tough in contrast to the 24x7 life of independence and self reliance in Mumbai.

Sensing my boredom, I was offered a small space in my own house to start off any business and keep myself occupied. I had always enjoyed the company of children, and so with the constraint of being at home, the obvious choice was to open a pre-school and an after-school hobby centre. I established a preschool called Tiny Tots. After 4 years or so, I was carrying my first (and only) born son Vrishin in my womb.

My journey of education was intertwined with parenting to a large extent. What started off as a Tiny tots pre-school grow into a Eurokids franchisee. I further continued on that path with Vibgyor to open up a grade school TIERRA in an upcoming locality of Bangalore of the time. While I worked my way through from a small home based preschool to a grade school, Vrishin was growing up alongside. I chose to keep him out of my owned schools to disallow any special treatment or focus, but he would spend time with me in my school during most afternoons after his own school got over.

A major illness of the gut struck me when my school was flourishing. While I recovered from it, circumstances made me lose most of what I had built in the past 17 years of my professional career. The illness not only impacted my financial and professional set-up, it took a huge physical and psychological toll on me. Doctors took months to even find out what was wrong. It would hurt so much to lie down that I'd keep walking for hours and hours, until my legs would walk no more. But as soon as I would lie down, the pain would return.

With the help of western science, meditation, yoga and homeopathy, but mostly by the grace of God, which came to me in form of my friends, I gradually but slowly recovered from my illness. And I knew I needed to get back to work to keep myself engaged. I had always been a business owner, but at this juncture of my life, I had nothing but my experience and a bunch of professional certifications I had cared to obtain in the past 17 years, thanks to my inclination for always learning new things.

When I met people in social gatherings, I found people who were immensely successful financially, but deeply unhappy. I also found people who were very talented and academically qualified, but with little financial success and respect from society. I started wondering what the cause of their suffering was, and started doing counseling and image consulting to help individuals transform into a bigger, better whole. People who would achieve success in all – social, emotional, financial, personal and professional – spheres of life.

Around this time, I also started consulting other pre-school owners to set-up and manage pre-schools and lead them to a path of profitability. I also met a young IITian named Rajat Toshniwal. Charged with a mission of making education more engaging and meaningful for children, Rajat invited me to join his group and develop curricula for children of grades 3-5. I chose to join him because of his passion towards teaching and learning.

From owning a business to consulting was an interesting shift of role. I was able to see things from far out and understand challenges of different stakeholders involved at different levels.

Slowly, my ties with Rajat grew further and we have are now in the process of setting up a new educational institution, which I'll write more about in the subsequent sections.

Parenting:

Some of my strongest emotional memories are of times shared with Vrishin. It is amazing how this mother-child bond can generate such a wide variety of emotions from joy to frustration, gratitude to anxiety, elation to fear... a never-ending list!

While my experiences with my child might not have been unique, a few learnings drawn from them are worth outlining.

1. **Being Around** - Vrishin loved to explore his physical world. My training in early childhood education enabled me to create a wide variety of environments for him. Be it spending time in a sand pit, or working with a variety of colours, or reading stories out of illustrated books, spending time with Vrishin helped me see what made him curious, happy, excited, sad, angry, etc. It helped me learn about his preferences and dislikes, and helped me connect with him deeply. And it also helped me learn how kids learn, that helped me create new, more interesting learning

experiences for him and other children at school.

2. **Being There** – As Vrishin continued to grow older, he needed me much less, atleast to take care of himself. So while we could spend an entire day away from each other, every evening Vrishin would come to me to share the highlights of his day. His experiences, after all, were new to him. And I used to help him make sense of his experiences. This time was special. Both I and Vrishin came to know each other better, and also helped develop Vrishin's ability to talk about emotions. Years laters, during image consulting, I realized how men suppressed almost every emotion except anger, and how a low EQ held the most outstanding men into the grip of mediocrity, or led to broken families and relationships. I hindsight, I think giving Vrishin a voice to express his emotions was the best thing I did for him.

3. **Being Different** – Right from the childhood, I could notice Vrishin having different tastes and preferences. He likes loud music, I prefer ghazals. He likes playing out in the field and watching movies, I love my books. I never sought to make him my mirror. I knew that to allow him to find his own identity, I needed to expose him to much more than what I liked to experience in my life. I have attended rock concerts with him, watched hundreds of silly Bollywood movies, cheered him when he's playing football on the field. By being around Vrishin, I have always tried to let him know that I do love him, irrespective of his choices. But more importantly, I have tried to expose him to the whole wide world, to help him make his own choices and find his own identity.

All in all, replacing judgment and expectations with curiosity and mindfulness helped me form a bond with Vrishin that more than filled up for my absence for long hours during the day thanks to my busy schedule in school management.

On Education:

While our society sees this differently, I believe education and parenting are two sides of the same coin. There cannot be good education without parenting. As the saying goes:

"Children never do what is told, but always do what they see."

If the above wasn't true, we could just program children like robots and schools won't be necessary any more. But if what children are told in schools is not what they see in their real life, then children simply will not take what is taught to them in schools.

1. **Role Models, not Teachers:** Children, therefore, need role models, both in school and at home. In my experience with preschool and later in grade school, I met so many parents who'd be doing cushy corporate jobs and staying in high rise buildings around the school, but who lacked even the most basic mannerisms and tact when it came to dealing with conflict. Faced with a difference in opinion, parents would write hate emails to me full of words they'd be horrified if their children would use. Yet, they expect schools to make sure their children become fine citizens. Without role modeling at home, good education in schools is impossible.

2. **Feedback, Not Judgment:** Children also need someone who would provide encouragement and feedback, without judgment. Consider this example: A students walks into a school 10 minutes past scheduled time. This child has been coming late to school 4-5 times every month. Here are three responses the teacher offers:

"You're late again! I will file a complaint with the principal if you are late next time!"

"Son, I have been seeing you have been coming late fairly often. Is something wrong? How can we help you being on time to school?"

"Class, here comes the late comer! You can please stand out till I finish this call, and no games for you today."

"No problem child. You can come in and take your seat."

What response did you get in your school? What response is your child getting in his/her school? Which response do you think is ideal?

Over the past few decades, we have gone from being oppressive and judgmental (responses 1 and 3) to permissive (response 4), while we need to be attentive (response 2). A great way to evaluate your child's school is to do this simple 'go late' test.

I taught all my teachers to be firm and fair. We need to hold students accountable, but also assist them in areas they are weak in. Punishments or ignorance does not lead to learning, but love and feedback do!

3.   **Life Skills, Not Exams:** Consider the most complex problems of your life right now. Have you been hoping to lose weight for years now? Do you and your spouse fight once every week? Has your boss been cruel to you, holding your promotion for 2 years in a row? Have you been struggling with management of your finances? Whatever your problem, now think of one thing that your schooling taught in over 15 years that can help you today to solve those problems? Could you recall anything? If you weren't, you are not alone.

Preparing children for life is not a goal of schools. Schools prepare children for exams, and exams in our schools are nothing like the exams real life challenges us with. Is there a way we can prepare children for life? Absolutely! Hundreds and thousands of books have been written on these subjects, and many can be made accessible for children. But since these cannot be tested on pen and paper, schools do not strive to teach them.

4. Ownership, Not Curricula: The fourth, and probably the most important aspect of education, is providing age appropriate challenges to students. Why? At your workplace, has monotony ever bored you? Imagine if your supervisor decided everything you'd do in a day, the moment you walked in to when you walked out? Children feel just the same in school. There's a lack of clear purpose and motivation, and without motivation, learning does not happen. Children need challenges that motivate them, so that they can own the learning process.

In my school, I keep these four as pillars of good education. Sure, children need to read books and clear examinations, but if the school pursues those goals at a loss of these ones, it is more likely to produce children that might succeed in their careers but fail in life.

The Future of Schooling:

So how do I plan to go forward from here? Along with Rajat, I plan to start Oogway Miscroschool, which we also refer to as the 'School of Wellness', an institution which will invest all its efforts equipping children with the right tools and skills to live well and perform well in this globally connected, rapidly changing, multi-cultural, multi-lingual world.

How would these schools be different from the regular grade schools? Here are a few differences you might find if you visit one:

- Supplemental: The schools we wish to set-up would not substitute grade school. These would be supplemental to the mainstream education. Requiring the child to spend only 4-10 hours a week, the school would exclusively focus on aspects of education that traditional schools consider less important.

- Small Scale: These schools would typically involve very few children. A class might have no more than 15 students, and most would have between 5-7. This would allow for high level of personalization.

- Accessible and Low Cost: The school would be operated within traditional schools or apartment complexes, making it easy for children to enrol in these schools. They will also be very cost effective to make it affordable for more and more parents to help this children learn with us.

- Exposure to New Trends: Our school would offer unique, real life experiences to children that traditional schools consider secondary. With basics of artificial intelligence to experiencing mindfulness and meditation, this medley of unique experiences will help children look closely at the real world and also find their own area of passion!

- Excellence Driven: Drawing from their exposure to new trends, all students in our schools would be required to pursue a pet project focused on making a contribution to the society. The projects would be entirely choice based to ensure students pursue only streams that motive them. Rajat already heads such an effort in the space of science education called Eureka STEM Club. By encouraging students to go for excellence, the aim to make them own and apply their classroom learning into a larger than life project and appreciate the complexity of real life.

- Student Directed: Unlike traditional schools, the most unique (and for most parents, most unsettling) aspect would be student ownership. Each child would make and follow his or her own calendar, and enjoy great flexibility in what he/she wants to do in any given time in our school.

- Balance Oriented: Students in these schools will be encouraged to develop a balanced and healthy life. They would evaluate their progress on areas as diverse as health, relationships, money management, emotional well being, etc. Students will be encouraged to adopt new practices to improve their overall well being and happiness.

- Portfolio Focused: The school would have no space for pen and paper tests. Rather, students would be required to make extensive portfolios of their work, which will make them accountable for the time spent in this school of wellness. The portfolio would track not only professional, but also other goals designed for relationships, health, behavior, etc.

We're already in discussion with a popular chain of schools in Bangalore to set up our first such school that will be launched in May 2017.

If you like my ideas around parenting and schooling, or you'd have some questions, feel free to write to me on amidesaiicbi@gmail.com. I would love to hear your questions and feedback.

Ami Desai

I am an innovative and conscientious entrepreneur started Tierra learning Pyramid in 1996. I aspire for new and challenging role that will offer development and progression in the field of Education and Training and develop my existing skill set too. I am highly dedicated Educator and a trainer with 19 years of experience who is passionate about Training and Learning.

Was a Director of leading Pre-School and High School

Provided an accelerated learning approach for children, giving young learners an early advantage early. Merged new discoveries in the teaching and learning domain with tried and tested play way approach. And from past 4 years I have started a Teacher Training Program and image management program – where I extend my expertise to train aspiring teachers.

Education

Institution Course Details University of Mumbai B.Sc in Statistics with Mathematics and Physics Cambridge University, UK Professional Diploma for Trainers and Teachers ICFAI University

Post Graduate Diploma in Finance Management iDiscoveri Education in partnership with Wipro Exercising Leadership in Schools Banjara Academy International Graduate Diploma in Counseling Skills; Certification in Student Counselling

In addition to the above, I have certifications in NTT, GNIIT, of working with ADD children, as a soft skills trainer, a train-the-trainer, a handwriting analyst, on story telling, phonics, power yoga, financial management and others. Awaiting Image Management Certification from Image Consulting Businesses Institute, Bangalore.

Social worker, have been a president in lioness club, active member of CSB and Harmony which promotes girl literacy across Bangalore. I conduct various workshops on parenting, teacher development programs, teenager and parent workshops, out bound workshops for school leaders, knowing beyond one self and much more.

I believe in providing a nurturing, supportive learning environment for children and adults that promotes image for success, problem solving, risk-taking, leadership and active inquiry.

My approach is using scientific tools to understand the need of my client and using this era's therapies, which includes:

- Multiple intelligence approach - where intelligence differentiates into specific (primarily sensory) "modalities", rather than seeing intelligence as dominated by a single general ability.

- Image consulting - is the process of empowering clients to reflect or project the confidence and competence that comes from an authentic, appropriate and attractive appearance for any personal, social or professional situation — to dress with substance and style.

• Soft skill enhancement program - It deals with educating, coaching, guiding and mentoring people by applying the art and science of soft skills and helping them lead a happier, more meaningful and successful life.

• Art therapy - The tenets of art therapy involve humanism, creativity, reconciling emotional conflicts, fostering self-awareness, and personal growth.

• Music therapy - is one of the expressive therapies, consisting of a process in which we use music and all of its facets—physical, emotional, mental, social, aesthetic, and spiritual—to help clients improve their physical and mental health.

• Grapho therapy - This is the practice of changing a person's handwriting with the goal of changing features of his or her personality.

Currently:
• Director –Tierra learning Pyramid
• Director –Bloom Grooming and Finishing School
• Consulting Preschools – training on marketing, selling, financial management and other areas
• Head of training, project head and architect of STEMSEA project 3-5 grades with Fitkids Education (DiscoverEd)
• Working with detective company on handwriting analysis
• Consulting clients on one-one image management
• Counseling teenagers and adults on life skills

Tierra learning Pyramid
643,7th block,11th cross, Jaynagar, Bangalore 560070
amidesaiicbi@gmail.com / +919886132043
www.bloomme.in

15

ARE YOU JUMPING OUT OF BED IN THE MORNING?
- BY DIANA DENTINGER, INSPIRATIONAL SPEAKER & FOUNDER OF THE MEANING OF LIFE SCHOOL

Do you jump out of bed in the morning, ready to happily face the day and excited to get to work?

Or are you lying in bed after the alarm goes off, dreading to have to go through another day, another trip to the office, another series of tasks that mean very little to you? Or are you somewhere in between, but realizing that you have to spend those 8 plus hours doing a "job" just so you can pay your bills?

Waking up with dread in the morning, doesn't sound like a lot of fun and isn't how most people want to live their lives. I'm willing to bet you don't either. I bet that you want to wake up with a burning desire to do something significant with your life. And that that something positively impacts those around you.

How to Move From Dread to Desire

Moving from "dread" to "desire" is a process and there are many steps along the way. The very first, and most vital one, is to mentally define, visually see and emotionally feel your Life Purpose.

This makes all the difference in quality of your day and the personal satisfaction you gain while moving forward along your path in life. Sure, there will always be some tasks that belong on the "have to do list" that you are less thrilled about, but with a clear Life Purpose, you have a more relaxed approach with them.

Maybe you are someone who already looks forward to going to work everyday but you'd like to live it more passionately, instead of having the rollercoaster of some good days and some bad. After 25 years of Corporate Training and Personal Development Coaching, I highly suggest to make "Finding your Life Purpose" a priority as soon as possible.

Without a heart felt Life Purpose, you think you are being held back by things "outside" of you, as if they had "power over you". Remember, your power comes from within you, but until you have unwavering clarity you get easily distracted, waste your time, and make choices based on external factors.

With a well grounded Life Purpose, you emanate a solid presence that radiates proactive energy. People want to be with you and opportunities come your way easily so you can express more of your Life Purpose. There is more flow to your life, and less resistance. It's physics!

By spending time on this first essential step and you will find that all of a sudden you can't wait to jump out of bed in the morning. You can't wait to get to work and time flies well past 5pm because it all feels so rewarding. When you're living your Life Purpose, you are fulfilling something deep within yourself and also making a difference in other people's lives.

When you aren't totally doing what you are here to do, then you are actually Subtracting that from a bigger picture of social contribution. Adding you at your best makes your life more fun and work isn't just work. It's something that you look forward to doing. Pause and ask yourself now what you really love to do, what you are great at doing and what is useful for others!

I created a personality profile and coaching process that gives people the exact answers to these questions by describing their innate desires and talents. Then I take them through a rapid process to define their Life Purpose. It requires first filling out a brief Questionnnaire so I elaborate the results. My mission is to help people spend more time living their purpose, and less time in finding their purpose.

How to Move From Working Your Purpose to Being Your Life Purpose

Since you, like most people from their mid twenties to sixties, dedicate the vast majority of their time "working a job", you realize that your overall life satisfaction depends on how much you feel aligned with who you are and why you are here. And if you are in the right place to express the best of yourself. As a psychosomatic illnesss therapist, as well as trained Coach, I have a deeper understanding and scientific approach to how people really function. I see the physical health consequences of them not having a Life Purpose. This includes having the answers to vital questions: Who am I, Why am I here and Where best can I serve.

Too many people are simply going through the motions of life, disconnected from their Life Purpose and overly conditioned by others. This has them living someone else's life path and losing themselves in the process. They dread or half dread their work week with very little sparkle in their eyes and in their hearts.

There are no better self-motivators than a clear Life Purpose together with a list of fulfilling Desires. These become the unstoppable forces that assist you in living happily and healthily. You have more vitality because these generate energy from within you and therefore you show up more confidently and get things done more efficiently. And this is a lot more powerful than any pressure from a boss or the promise of financial rewards.

After completing step one, you move to step two where you remember that you are a human being. As it seems easier to observe yourself "doing" your Life Purpose in the "visible" way through your actions and the results you achieve in your career or profession, now observe yourself outside of work.

How do you feel? What do you dream about? What more do you you want from life? If money and time were out of the recipe, what ingredients would you mix together to cook up a fantastic life?

Along your path of life, work is just a part. You have a relationship with yourself, you take care of yourself. You have relationships with others. These go from being intimate ones to familiar to acquaintances. You bring yourself in every relationship, even to the book you read and the water you swim in.

When you mentally define, visually see and emotionally feel your Life Purpose in your work, it is just a facet. What about how you are, think and act when you are shopping, exercising, cleaning up or on vacation.

Your Life Purpose is you in every moment, everywhere and with everyone. There is no separation between work and play, between paid time and free time. When you are in the picture, you bring your Life Purpose with you because it is the core of everything you feel, say and do. It is your big why always.

It's More About Life than Just Work

We are social creatures with a conscience. That means it's important to us to touch the lives of those around us in a meaningful way. Think about it... doesn't it make you feel good when you can do a favor for someone else?

There's a reason behind the "Random Acts of Kindness" movement. Have you ever read stories about people who pay things forward, offering a meal or coffee to the next person in line at a coffee shop? We do things because it makes us feel good.

Your Life Purpose is not just what you do, but actually why you do it.

It is the reason why something moves you from the inside and drives you deeply to perform an action. But as I stated before, many people are on auto drive. They are less conscious of what and why they do certain things. And being in a hurry, and less aware, they feel "random" happiness. They yearn for the feeling of fulfillment, when in fact their life is quite empty.

Without a reason, a meaning, a Life Purpose, life can be seen as empty. In this day and age of wanting, we tend to fill that void with things, instead of being "full of ourselves".

You living your Life Purpose is the most fulfilling thing and you won't find it on the outside. It gives you the inner peace to sleep restfully and be excited to jump out of bed each and everyday, even on weekends.

It is fine now if you are dreading the day to day routine, or if you feel it could be a bit daunting to step onto a fuller life path. It is worth your time and effort to pause, ask yourself what is truly meaningful for you and answer the questions throughout the article. Your Life Purpose is a process of unravelling so you live the greater meaning of why you are here for greater health and happiness.

Diana Dentinger

Diana has been an Entrepreneur, Corporate Team Building Specialist and Executive Coach for over 25 years, certified in and using the main stream behavior assessments up until the year 2000. Finding them incomplete and outdated she created a 21st Century Performance Profile shortly after. The Personality & Needs Profile™ skyrockets your self awareness and catalyzes long lasting change for profound personal happiness, better health and greater success.

Diana grew up on an enormous family of over 250 relatives in the midwest of America. Her curiosity about human behavior started as a child noticing among cousins the difference between siblings. Diana even observed her tens of aunts and uncles in their differing parenting styles using some as role models for her own family. She knew in her heart that there must be a way to describe the diversity of interests, talents and values that each one excelled. That way there could be even more support and understanding in families and in the work place. To create this tool, Diana spent years in rigorous, scientific brain research, studying with top European Sociologists, Anthropologists and Psychologists to become a neurobiology therapist unblocking the causes of psychosomatic illnesses. She is also specialized in Etymology, the mind's Key Word Coding and ancient Symbology.

Applying the biological principles of the brain and advanced research about human programming, Diana found the key to unlock the potential in your DNA. The Profile and related Coaching Programs give you instant confidence, connectedness and courage to live your life's work, while maintaining balance. Plus you have the tools to finally strategize your unique way to achieve success without the risk of losing yourself along the way.

Diana's Keynote Speeches focus on the importance of being who you really are. She says: "No one could teach you how to be you... until now". She feels she is that teacher. "Most people settle for less, not because their dream is too big or they don't have the resources, but because they don't know how to access what is already inside of them."

Diana elaborated both the leading edge Personality & Needs Profile™ as well as her proprietary Coaching Programs to meet the needs of both the left and the right brainers. She combines the necessary, logical explanations together with creative drawing and game playing. Her clients love the freshness of her approach.

Her programs are available as VIP in Person Intensives, Group Workshops and Personalized Online E-Learning Portals.

American born in Chicago, Illinois, Diana has lived over 30 years in Europe raising her 4 children in northern Italy. In her free time she loves to travel, dance. Get ready to achieve more in your life, relationships and work simply by being yourself.

16

IMBIBING QUALITY AS A WAY OF LIFE
-BY VANISHREE P ACHARYA, MANAGING DIRECTOR OF KROMASPECTS SCITEC SOLUTIONS PVT. LTD.

During my nearly two-and-a-half decade tenure in the Pharmaceutical industry in various roles, I was constantly exposed to the mismatch between the available talent pool and the required talent pool. The human resources lacked the skills that the recruiters were seeking. This is when I thought, in the year 2002 why not bridge this gap through training -- training people in skills that were required by the industry to make them ready, from an employability perspective. The time to plunge from being an employee to becoming an entrepreneur was ripe for several personal reasons. I was then working at Syngene International Pvt. Ltd., a subsidiary of Biocon as a Senior Scientific Associate. I was responsible for testing newly developed products and was part of a large team. The role I played required me to put in long hours and my family was feeling the brunt of my absence. I somehow felt that I was not doing justice to both family and career. However, I did not want to give up on my career completely either. I was looking for a way to stay in touch with the industry.

In 2002, I launched my company Kromaspects to offer consultation and training in quality for the pharmaceutical sector. The primary aim of my organization is to support the pharmaceutical industry in quality aspects. I started my career as a Quality Control Executive in Cipla. By the time I exited Syngene, I had 11 years of experience in this domain. When I launched training for the industry, I was way ahead of the market and of the times. When training was finally considered a prerequisite to enable and update human resources, I had a clear distinction of being one of the earliest players in the market, and thus I was hailed a thought leader in the training industry. Currently, we are addressing the growing need for training in the field of Analytical Instrumentation for the Chemical, Pharmaceutical and Bio-Pharmaceutical Industries. Employees in such certified and regulated industries need to be highly efficient and capable of handling and delivering accurate results even under the most demanding of conditions and stringent regulatory requirements. Hence, all aspects related to quality systems in these industries fall within the scope of training and consulting. However, you may have in place the most efficient systems and best practices, but if the mental and emotional well-being of your employees is not addressed, nothing will work. Hence, our training has two aspects: one is imparting technical know-how and the other is initiating the process of self-awareness and self-healing.

Self-healing

All of us are leading stressed lives. We are under tremendous pressure round the clock: to shoulder responsibilities, maintain a certain lifestyle, juggle roles, multi-task, the list is endless. Before all of this takes a toll on our mental and physical health, it is better to be aware and prevent ill health. I strongly believe in the adage, prevention is better than cure. The tendency is to watch a problem as it arises, grows and becomes full-blown. All the while, we do not get into action mode to nip it in the bud. Only when the problem begins to overwhelm us, we try to address it. By then, the issue would have become too complex, and sorting it would take up too much of our time, mental and emotional resource and money. It is always easier and wiser to address a problem in the initial stages. Hence, I did a lot of research in the science of alternative healing. I also understood the concept of left-brain approach and right-brain approach to problem solving and healing. The right brain is inclined towards a creative and intuitive approach, whereas the left-brain is inclined towards a logical and scientific approach. The left brain can take you up to the knowledge zone. This zone, however, is limited to the knowledge that you gain from the external world. The intuitive zone is far more powerful as it helps look within your own self for knowledge and for answers. Meditation, I learned, is one technique that really empowers you with ways of discovering yourself and healing yourself. I also explored Reiki and Pranic healing techniques. I learned different forms of meditation. Having learned music from a very young age and being particularly receptive to auditory stimulation, I was attracted to various musical tracks and guided meditation exercises. I intuitively connected with Tibetan Sound Bowl Meditation, one of the most powerful forms of meditation. I learned this form of Meditation and healing from Sujata Singhi from Mumbai, who was directly initiated by the Lama gurus. I am now one of the professional healers in Bangalore who provide healing through sound and we have worked with a lot of people for stress relief and block removals.

The good thing is that our generation is in the middle of a wellness and personal development revolution. People are open to discovering themselves. Now, why am I stressing so much on self-healing? Because, the knowledge that we transfer is common, standard. However, every recipient processes knowledge in different ways. Each has to find his or her own method and process of self-healing. This is a diluted echo of a very great philosophical thought of the Buddha. The Buddha says: "Work out your own salvation. Do not depend on others."

The pharma industry is engaged in the task of enhancing the wellness of the society. It is imperative that the human resources working in this industry are healthy themselves to ensure optimal output. If the resources are not in the right frame of mind, then the very vision of the pharma industry -- wellness of society -- is threatened.

Three-pronged approach to Quality

1. Quality is a Mindset

Quality is not a task or a role that an employee plays. It is a commitment towards oneself; to achieve a state of being where you can give your maximum. When I talk about quality, I am not referring to a tangible product-quality but a measure of one's own excellence. Are you putting in your best? That is the question. If not, what do you have to do to optimize yourself?

2. Quality is Reliability

Reliability is a measure of how consistently you can utilize yourself optimally. Only if quality becomes a mindset, can you be reliable. A relationship can be sealed only if you can consistently offer quality.

3. Quality is Safety

So if you can deliver quality, consistently, then safety is achieved. Ultimately, safety is the most important feature of a product. A product's look and feel may be great; it may function very well too, but if it is not safe to use, then the product is bound to fail sooner or later.

Thus, quality is a built-in feature. It is inherent and integral to our very being. If it is a cosmetic layer, it will not last long. It will not be consistent, for it alters with changing circumstances. Quality is like an unyielding constant; everything around it may change. But it remains.

Now, having said that, how does one enhance the quality of one's life? Quality becomes a mindset only when applied to all aspects of life. If, for instance, you, as an employee, are functioning optimally at work, but neglecting your personal well-being, then over a period of time, your overall quality will drop. A holistic approach to quality life is what the current generation is missing.

To understand lifestyle and wellness in the Indian context, I am conducting extensive research into the Typical Indian Mindset (TIM). As a culture, we are sometimes laidback about crucial etiquette: punctuality, work ethic, a sense of orderliness, the list is endless.

Here are a few simple things you can do to enhance the quality of your life:

1. **Meditate every day for at least 10 to 15 minutes.** Spending time watching television or reading a book is not the same as meditating. Selfish 'me-time' is different from 'selfless me-time'. Meditation is a way of giving complete rest to the mind. It is a state of stillness to connect to your inner-self. Meditation initiates introspection and actualization. I am looking forward to becoming a certified meditation instructor. Practicing meditation opened a floodgate of possibilities for me. It is a particularly effective tool for prevention of lifestyle and wellness related issues.

2. **Exercise mindfulness as a conscious process.** Observe your thoughts, your actions, and your words. Enhance the level of your awareness about yourself and the environment around you; the various stimuli that are being perceived by your senses, and your responses to them.

3. **Take up every task with utmost commitment;** be it small or big; important or trivial. Circumstances and people around you may change. Your commitment should not waver.

These three attitudes form the crux of the intuitive approach to enhancing quality. If you want a more tangible quantitative feedback, several psychometric tests are available to measure your quality index. Tools such as MBTI (questionnaire to indicate psychological preferences of people) fingerprint test analysis (DMIT) and handwriting analysis also give an insight into your quality index and suggest ways enhance quality.

At my organization, we use a combination of intuitive and scientific approaches to evolve a comprehensive understanding of your personality and create a unique road map to help you embark on the next level of your life's journey.

My dream and vision is to see India re-emerge as a Super power and Knowledge capital of the World. The best way to do this is to re-instate many of the ancient Indian Sciences, Culture and Heritage in a way that the today's generation can perceive and understand. To achieve this, I have been volunteering for the activities of National Institute of Vedic Sciences Trust, teaching children about Ancient Chemistry and participating in their International Conferences on Ancient Indian Sciences.

I strongly believe that gratitude is a very great mindset, as it is an externalization of humility and it enriches you in amazing ways. For all that society has given to me, I want to give back something too. I have volunteered for CMCA (Children's movement for Civic Awareness) where I worked with children to improve their civic sense and lead them on a path to active citizenship.

As Ralph Waldo Emerson says, 'Cultivate the habit of being grateful for every good thing that comes to you, and to give thanks continuously. And because all things have contributed to your advancement, you should include all things in your gratitude.'

Vanishree P Acharya

Vanishree P Acharya has spent more than 25 years in domain of Quality and analysis of Pharmaceutical products.

She has predominantly been in the area of Analytical Research, QC and QA and has covered diverse activities including Method development, Validations , Documentation and Implementation of quality systems. Her experience in the area of Computerised systems validations and equipment qualifications is very significant and this domain expertise supports a lot of pharma vendors to position their products effectively.

She has also spent more than 14 years in training many pharmaceutical professionals to develop their skills in the area of Pharmaceutical Analysis and Quality methodologies."

She is a Certified Quality Auditor and Certified Manager of Quality and Organisational Excellence from the American Society of Quality.

She is passionate about Helping Entrepreneurs and Small Enterprises set up their Quality systems and processes in an innovative and sustainable manner. Her dream and vision is to Enhance Quality of life in a simplistic manner. She is keen on achieving this through promoting meditation and integrated healing techniques for holistic health and wellbeing.

17

HOW CONSULTATIVE FINESSE BEATS TYPICAL FIGHT VS. FLIGHT IN STRESSFUL WORK SITUATIONS

-BY ROLF FOSTER-JORGENSEN, GLOBAL CONSULTING AUTHORITY, CERTIFIED HIGH PERFORMANCE COACH, AWARD-EARNING FACILITATOR/TRAINER

Think back to a time when you felt embarrassed at work. Perhaps a boss disciplined or someone else ridiculed your work, or you just said something on a group call that you wished could have been retracted and erased from everyone's memory. I'm not trying to make you feel discouraged, as everyone has had similarly unpleasant experiences. It's difficult to deny that it was stressful and hurt, even if you rationalize that the conflict made you stronger. Truthfully, those are instances where our inner drive kicks in to want to either fight or flee.

My older brother passed away a few years ago and, though I loved him dearly, there was no denying that he struggled all his life to hold a steady job. The main reason was because he was brilliant, at least as measured by IQ tests. Now you may say how can a brilliant person really struggle when that should open many doors? The problem was that something always happened that exposed his feeling smarter than his boss, and he failed to learn how NOT to say so. Anyone could easily get fired after telling a boss that he or she is stupid, right? Classic "fight" scenario, eh?

I know. You say that you've learned greater self-discipline to not get fired that way. Even if you said something that was perceived to be rude, yet not bad enough to get fired, there was likely some immediate verbal or nonverbal feedback about inappropriate behavior. However, think back to times when you may NOT have said anything, even when you knew you were right, particularly if others acted forcefully in those situations. Choosing NOT to speak up about your insights and opinions is a form of "fleeing". For those working in a friendly, supportive environment, it may not seem to be an issue, yet trying to measure the intangible career impact of "fleeing" inaction can be difficult unless there were a way to bring it to your attention.

Do you ever wish you had some tools to better understand what, why and how others are likely to act BEFORE a situation escalates to a fight vs. flight decision? That is where the online and face-to-face Consultative Skills methods I've designed and developed over 30+ years provide a safer, middle ground. It's the FINESSE sitting between Fight vs. Flight options, that you can subtly apply without fanfare or disruption that may feel uncharacteristic to how you prefer to work.

In fact, that is how I work best, quietly behind the scenes, helping others look good in a respectful, discrete, confidential manner. Before you judge that as not your style, please understand it was not always mine either. I'm living proof that anyone can learn to be a subtle influencer.

For background, I'm an unassuming Canadian who grew up in the US in a functional family of two parents and two siblings. My Father was a Lutheran pastor and Mother a part-time bookkeeper, happily married since age 25. While that may sound boring, it certainly did not seem so to me. My Dad loved variety, a trait I thankfully learned to embrace and instill in our children. About every 2-6 years, my Dad would accept a different "call" (how you moved in the church). They varied from inner city to suburban, rural to international, start-up congregations to established multi-lingual institutions. He was the first US exchange pastor in Oslo because he spoke fluent Norwegian. Upon arrival, he was surprised when told that sermons were expected to be 3+ hours long. I was only 8, so I thought EVERY Dad did public speaking as their job. That helped me naturally develop the confidence to act, sing, play timpani/ percussion, and serve others as a professional consultant/ trainer/ facilitator.

I earned a Bachelor of Arts four-year Liberal Arts degree in Political Science with Urban Studies Concentration (minor) from a prestigious and rigorous school. Yet that included changing my major five times before settling on what was more popular at the time than my real passion for business. The PolySci degree included internships at government bureaucracies and with national political leaders during particularly scandalous times (when isn't there, eh?). Disillusioned, I accepted a job with a global not-for-profit business education organization, youthfully rationalizing that I would at least be idealistically "helping people". I quickly realized that political science knowledge applied wherever there were groups forming to influence others. I was honoured that others identified me for fast-track training, catapulting over more seasoned staff to become the organization's youngest staff president (the title used in only the top 25 markets). In that role, I hired excellent staff, recruited and served a high-level board of directors of Fortune 500 C-Suite executives, and authored the then largest national grant from a major foundation. I learned a lot about executives, including that they put their pants on the same as anyone else and you just need to proactively anticipate their needs while wisely using their time and influence. Some of them helped me start my consulting practice when only age 30. Still, I wish someone had shown that immature me some quick and effective tools such as I've recently developed. My economical SituationalALERTness℠ online video training available 24/7 helps to anticipate how and why subgroups are likely to act BEFORE you might need their support or lack of resistance. My CHALLENGE execYOUtives℠ online program guides you through various levels of consultative wording for respectfully and safely challenging a boss, or anyone in authority, in ways that enhance your career.

I've often been asked how can I be a "consultant" without grey hair or a Ph.D.? Yes, I've subcontracted many with those credentials onto my teams when a client seemed initially nervous. Yet that usually only initially propped open a door. They understandably also ask, "What are you doing to help me today?" Quite frankly, I've proven that practical real life experience that unselfishly fosters insight and wisdom also earns trust and respect…and repeat business.

Did I test my limits along the journey? Definitely. My wife and I have started, acquired and sold numerous businesses, including multi-million dollar ones with up to 150 employees. She proved to have greater patience than I when dealing with some of our managers who did not see things that needed to be done with their direct reports, even after being told what to do. I finally realized that my trying to "tell" them what to do was the root cause of their not following through once I left the premises to visit our other locations. Why would they internalize and implement MY processes when my only consistency was to criticize and press for faster results?

Ironically, that was not the way I was simultaneously treating my consulting clients in the early years of our mainstay business. No, I consultatively coached, good humoredly challenged, and gently guided them toward committing to their own priorities. In fact, that was so successful that it led me to a major epiphany. Why not treat EVERYONE that way and no longer feel stressed about others seemingly letting ME down. Plus, consistently applying consultative behaviours with everyone meant not having to remember what was said to whom as nothing harmful would come back to bite me later.

Do Yourself a F.A.V.O.U.R.

Now, whenever I feel any negativity toward anything, I apply a simple process I call, "Do Yourself a F.A.V.O.U.R." (Yes, it's Canadian spelling). It stands for
:
F = Feel   Embrace your feelings, regardless of business style or situation

A = Acknowledge   Catch yourself as early as possible when thinking negatively

V = Value   Value every relationship more than any atypical incident or thought

O = Own It   Don't blame anyone else for your own reactions to any situation

U = Understand   Remember you're dealing with behaviours, not the whole person

R = Release   Give yourself permission to let it go, forgive yourself, and just move on

Thinking back, those struggling managers helped me learn an important life lesson.

"Deal with people wherever they are at the moment, and help them stretch at their own pace to whatever changes they are willing to consider."

That helped me create a safe enough space for many clients to proactively grow into true high performers. (I later became one of the founding 100 members of global High Performance Coaches, as certified by the High Performance Academy).

Most of my clients for decades have been Fortune 500 executives, managers and support roles. That has meant signing confidentiality, non-disclosure and non-compete agreements. It has also meant no internal video, pictures or written testimonials (per legal department advice about ANY outside resource) despite extensive praise and repeat business. That is often part of the trade-off when earning access to such confidential areas as intellectual property/ trade secrets, competitive/ business intelligence, strategic planning meetings, etc. When other consultants ask me how to get started, I sometimes joke, "Be careful what you wish for unless you're willing to also accept their rules." So why am I now sharing my insights here and via my consultativeskills.com website? I've learned how to teach skills to others without violating the confidence of my short and long term clients.

Act Authentically Without Airs

A colleague once introduced me to a group as "...the wisest person I know." I quickly asked if he spelled that "wisest" or "wise-assed"? They laughed and he responded, "Now that you mention it – both". It was a reminder not to take myself too seriously or let ego get in the way of serving others.

My professional gratification comes from seeing how others apply learning gained from my training, coaching and facilitating. Let's explore a few actual examples. One was somewhat simple and the other more complex. Watch for subtle examples of what I call "consultative finesse".

A coaching client once commented that she admired how her boss would be in a group meeting of direct reports and peers, and just intently listen to a discussion. Then he would add some profoundly deeper perspective that would take the group outside the narrow company point of view. Finally, he would pose the most insightfully crafted questions that would stop people in their tracks while they thought about their answers.

After teaching her how to craft consultative questions, I asked her how she thought her boss might respond if she chose to just be candid and express her desire to emulate those learned traits. Perhaps ask him what ezines and periodicals he regularly reads that might help her professionally grow and offer greater value to the team. On our next call, she excitedly reported that he responded by offering her a leadership role on an exciting new project and set up a formal mentoring process together.

It's always refreshing to see the business rewards that can result from a little simple initiative about being more open to self-improvement and learning.

In another case, I was brought in as an independent subject matter expert by the Learning Organization (LO) division of a major company to meet with who they claimed to be a "domineering and stubborn" Sr. VP. Before agreeing to the meeting, I learned that apparently they were having difficulty convincing the executive to invest in their proposed "solution" to a problem he had approached them to fix. Based on my years of successfully conducting "consultative skills" classes within the firm, their solution included just uplifting my proven services. So I was supposedly to be at the meeting to soften up the prospect toward their "off-the-shelf" approach, even though the methods I teach are to customize solutions to best meet the client's needs. In other words, the learning team just wanted to get rid of the request by conveniently outsourcing their solution to a proven "vendor" with the assumption that my classes would suffice. When I asked what "needs requirements" steps they had previously taken to understand the request before proposing this particular solution, I was told that they had seen the same situation so many times that they didn't "waste this important executive's time" by typically exploring internal client issues. I hope you see the root cause of their dilemma.

At the meeting, I quickly confirmed this prospective client's dominant style and knew he would have greater respect if I showed that I could take charge of the meeting and steer it toward meeting HIS needs, not necessarily the learning division's representatives. By consultatively asking some open-ended questions, we quickly identified the challenges being faced by the executive, how they were impacting accomplishing his business goals, and some preferred behavioral outcomes that might address the gaps. I thought about how obvious it was to me that by simply tweaking some of the scenarios, or even the rigorous case study I use in my class, we could accomplish dramatic improvements. However, I shocked the learning reps by saying to the client that, depending on how quickly he wanted sustainable results, there were multiple methods of accomplishing the altered behaviours that would likely achieve his business goals. These could include training, coaching, mentoring, etc. each with their own trade-offs to consider. Even though the LO's solution would help me as the fulfillment contractor, I did this because I knew his dominant style preferred multiple options and risks/rewards factors from which to choose.

One of the LO reps immediately jumped in, thinking he would help his team and me, by pointing out that I had the highest satisfaction rankings of any of their external AND internal trainers and the client "should" select my maximum 30-person 3-day Consultative Skills classes. Appearing to feel boxed in, the client stated that he thought the best approach was to have his assistant (who was also in the conference room with us) travel to the six geographies of his division and conduct single meetings of about 150 people so as to minimize their time "away from productive work". It was that conflict that had prompted the LO setting up this particular meeting involving me, hoping that I would simply endorse their idea of repeatedly using my services.

I saw the situation differently and chose to apply another consultative approach (for which the client later complimented me for role modeling what he really wanted his team to learn to do with external customers). After honoring the talents and good intentions of the assistant, I asked them both what might happen if a sizeable percentage of his team either did not fully understand their message, or chose not to implement it. After the client's initial reaction about people risking their careers by ignoring his mandates, I could see him pondering the question more deeply. I then switched the emphasis to a question about the potential impact to HIM if those less-than-committed team members undermined achieving his division quarterly or annual goals. When the client acknowledged how bad that would be, I asked his assistant whether he believed "compliance" was the same as "buy-in" on their extended team. They both said no, and that opened the door to explore alternatives.

Again, rather than only pitch the LO solution of using my classes, I instead stated one way to possibly increase buy-in, even with groups of 150+ people at a time, could be to use expert "facilitation" skills in order to guide, rather than force, people to voluntarily buy in. I asked the assistant what training, if any, he had experienced in learning and practicing expert facilitation skills. He said he had none, after which a different LO rep boldly stated that to be one of Rolf's strongest skills. While I appreciated the compliment, her timing was off. It seemed too risky to appear to be pitting my strengths as an outside expert whom the client had just met, against his already trusted assistant. I instead moved to a more face-saving approach for the assistant.

I intentionally asked a rare closed question of whether they believed people learned more and retained the learning better when they had the opportunity to personally interact with peers and promptly apply the learning to their jobs. Everyone agreed that was most desirable, provided it also met budget, time and other typical constraints. I then asked a "what if" question to help broaden perspectives about different alternatives. I asked, "What if I were to team up with the assistant, providing my consultative skills and facilitation expertise as an available supplement to the assistant's lead and knowledge of the audience and the client's priorities?" The signs of relief on the assistant's face were noticeable to all, yet I didn't stop there with the obvious compromise because I still knew the trade-offs of trying to train groups of 150+ people were unlikely to meet the desired business goals. I asked if everyone would prefer not allowing individual team members to "hide" amongst a large group and possibly ignore the message without anyone realizing it until after some quarterly goals were not met. They all agreed that was undesirable.

Their OWN REPLIES presented the opening to discuss some benefits of training in smaller conspicuous groups. While I acknowledged in a neutral way that I could use my instructional design experience to develop some educational activities for any size groupings, including 150+, I also walked them through some examples where greater levels of interaction, team-building and reinforced learning seemed to work better within smaller groups with a common vision, mission, and directly perceived benefits.

Then a few important things happened, primarily because they all seemed more comfortable by that time. The assistant asked his boss if it was OK for me (Rolf) to conduct all the training and he would supplement it, as a background resource should any technical questions arise about the company. I offered to customize some of the training exercises to use real-life situations that their team would recognize and appreciate. The client agreed to all that and also committed to trying the smaller classes at one of their sites as a test. By providing the assistant with a graceful way to choose to bow out of the training leadership role, it allowed me to then ask the client to prepare a 1-2 minute video embarking his vision and priorities that could be played during each class delivery.

As expected, that test went so well that the client committed to my conducting numerous other classes all over the globe, and the assistant told his boss that it was no longer necessary to tag along as I had demonstrated to their teams that I understood them well. The desired business results were also accomplished faster than expected as the learning was quickly applied within their roles.

There were also some other longer-term benefits. The LO reps said they learned a lot about how to deal better with other executives in the future, and kept renewing my contracts. The client also engaged me as his personal High Performance Coach. We're currently exploring how best to engage some of my fellow Certified High Performance Coaches for group coaching his teams across the globe.

Apply Good Judgment Without Appearing Judgmental
Unlike the examples above, many times I'm brought in to help facilitate a process as a neutral party with no connection to any outcomes. For example, a large client desired a systematic internal process to conduct market intelligence research that could also help

external customers. Working with my now-retired associate, Mike Kirkwood, we effectively facilitated a roll-up-your-sleeves workshop with internal stakeholders that produced a succinct process generating broad-based buy-in. Besides Mike having been a founding member of the International Association of Facilitators, the main reason we were brought in was because we had been teaching our own proprietary consultative skills model for years. Now, we certainly could have allowed that to skew our input yet understood how crucial it was to separate our judgment from what would have likely been construed as appearing "judgmental" if we had crossed that line. What are some ways where you might add greater value to a team or project by maintaining that balance between advocating your own judgment vs. appearing to be judgmental to others?

How might that distinction make a difference, you ask? After facilitating many groups experiencing all kinds of dynamics, I was honoured by a US$400 million training services firm as their top Facilitation Partner of the Year, the same year they earned the prestigious Malcolm Baldrige service award. I was later honoured by my peers and the global board to be one of two co-chairs of the 2015 Americas Conference of the International Association of Facilitators. More significantly for you, what situations are you or a team facing where a neutral professional facilitator may assist toward your creating a desired breakthrough? How might it be helpful for YOU to learn and apply consultative "finesse" in any and every work (or family) situation?

Whether you currently manage people or teams, and/or are subtly working your way up within any business culture, I invite you to contact me at info@optimire.com and visit www.consultativeskills.com for a complimentary video series and downloadable "Team Ethics Analysis Model" ebook. I have a ten-year business visa to work in India as well as regularly conduct long distance coaching and consulting engagements in many time zones.

Let's explore your needs together.

During my nearly three-decade tenure in the Pharmaceutical industry in various roles, I was constantly exposed to the mismatch between the available talent pool and the required talent pool. The human resources lacked the skills that the recruiters were seeking. This is when I thought, in the early 1990s, why not bridge this gap through training -- training people in skills that were required by the industry to make them ready, from an employability perspective. The time to plunge from being an employee to becoming an entrepreneur was ripe for several personal reasons. I was then working at Syngene International Pvt. Ltd., a subsidiary of Biocon as a Senior Scientific Associate. I was working long hours and my family was feeling the brunt of my absence. I also found it very stressful, for there was no way of doing justice to both family and career. However, I did not want to give up on my career

Rolf Foster-Jorgensen

President Optimire Consulting and Training, Inc.
Canmore AB Canada
info@optimire.com   www.ConsultativeSkills.com

Learn from Rolf's 30+ years as a global lead consultant, trainer, facilitator and Certified High Performance Coach to Fortune 500 clients and entrepreneurial teams.

- Rolf was awarded as the top "Facilitation Partner of the Year" by a US$400 million Malcolm Baldrige service award winner.

- He served as 2015 Co-Chair of the International Association of Facilitators Americas Conference.

- Rolf is an inaugural member of global Certified High Performance Coaches, and personally invited on stage twice by the High Performance Academy founder to share coaching tips based on his extensive experience and insights.

- Rolf provides interactive e-learning, rigorous case studies and participatory classroom instructional design services, and Train-The-Trainer (T3) events.

- He is creator and master facilitator of Consultative Skills, and co-creator of Internal Consultative Skills with marketing and communications emphasis.

- He authored Team Ethics Analysis Model ebook, and created the Business Empathy Tool, SituationalALERTness℠ and Challenge ExecYOUtive℠ products/services for all audiences.

- Rolf has also designed, developed, and delivered courses in consultative project planning, project management, market management, complex solutions selling, customer service, facilitation skills, leadership coaching and hardware/software planning.

- He and his wife owned multi-million dollar businesses with 150+ employees.

- Rolf 's hobbies include playing timpani and Latin percussion in various bands and orchestras as time permits.

Clients include: IBM, Cisco, General Motors, the International United Auto Workers Union, Chrysler, Ford-Volvo, BP/Amoco Oil, Navistar/International Truck & Engine/Monaco Coach, Hewlett-Packard, Yamaha, Abbott Labs, American Airlines/US Airways, Nissan-Infiniti, Motorola, Agilysys, Fluor, Pfizer, small businesses, state/municipal government, not-for-profits, Native Indigenous tribe.

Watch for early release notices about Rolf's upcoming Risk-Giving℠ book. It presents a different business operations model that greatly honours employees at every level, while encouraging high performance behaviours by all. People managers and team leaders, of any title, will particularly appreciate how collaboratively rewarding their roles can be in a Risk-Giving℠ environment.

ABOUT THE AUTHORS

This is a book written by industry experts, each contributing a chapter. Here's a list of all the CO-AUTHORS of this publication (in no particular order):

1 Shashidhar Jakkali
2 Phil Britten
3 C T Parun
4 Dr. Joanne Messenger
5 Savitha Hosmane
6 Sunitha
7 Johann Nogueira
8 Lisa Scolnick
9 Vishwanath Kokkonda
10 Amit Punjabi
11 Adrian Reid
12 Glenn Dietzel
13 Cydney O Sullivan
14 Ami Desai
15 Diana Dentinger
16 Vanishree Acharya
17 Rolf Foster-Jorgensen

www.ingramcontent.com/pod-product-compliance
Lightning Source LLC
Chambersburg PA
CBHW030918180526
45163CB00002B/385